THE COMPLETE
GUIDE TO REGIONAL
MARKETING

THE COMPLETE GUIDE TO REGIONAL MARKETING

Shawn McKenna

BUSINESS ONE IRWIN
Homewood, Illinois 60430

This publication is designed to provide accurate and
authoritative information in regard to the subject matter
covered. It is sold with the understanding that neither the
author nor the publisher is engaged in rendering legal, accounting,
or other professional service. If legal advice or other expert
assistance is required, the services of a competent
professional person should be sought.

*From a Declaration of Principles jointly adopted by a Committee
of the American Bar Association and a Committee of Publishers.*

Sponsoring editor:	Cynthia A. Zigmund
Project editor:	Rebecca Dodson
Production manager:	Ann Cassady
Designer:	Laurie Entringer
Artist:	Electronic Desktop Services
Compositor:	Alexander Graphics Limited
Typeface:	11/14 Palatino
Printer:	Arcata Graphics/Kingsport

Library of Congress Cataloging-in-Publication Data

McKenna, Shawn.
    The complete guide to regional marketing / Shawn McKenna.
      p.   cm.
    Includes index.
    ISBN 1-55623-422-8
    1. Marketing—Management.   I. Title   II. Title: Regional
marketing.
    HF5415.13.M3692   1991
    658.8'3—dc20   91–16564

Printed in the United States of America
1 2 3 4 5 6 7 8 9 0 AGK 8 7 6 5 4 3 2 1

DEDICATION

I want to dedicate this book on two levels, one personal, the other professional:

Personal—To my wife Deb and children Ryan, Erin, and Riley. I hope you now understand why I had to spend our weekends and vacations with a dictation unit and stacks of notes.

Professional—To Ton Vissers, who gave me plenty of freedom, guidance, and patience as I helped test and develop regional marketing for Procter & Gamble. Additionally, thanks for sharing with me your style of principled thinking.

Best Wishes

To all the friends and business associates that I developed during my several years with Procter & Gamble. Procter & Gamble is truly an outstanding company because of its people and, therefore, out of respect for its people, I worked hard to ensure that this book was not an exposé.

Foreword

When the manuscript of this book was delivered to my home on Hilton Head Island, South Carolina, I gave myself four days to read it, which was all the time I had before leaving for an extended trip out of the country. I completed it in one day! No, not because of time pressure, but because I found it to be the most enlightened, refreshing, and comprehensive treatise on the subject of regional marketing I have ever read.

As Mr. McKenna points out, regional marketing is not a new concept. In fact, practically every sales and marketing executive in business today can articulate a pretty good definition of the concept. However, only a handful can show you an effective regional marketing program actually operating in the marketplace. I believe there are a number of contributing factors for this, ranging from inertia, to internal power politics, to the ever-present human reluctance to change. But perhaps the single most important factor is management's adherence to the paradigm that all they have to do in the future is simply do what they have done in the past—just do it better.

To all those managers, Shawn McKenna sends a loud and clear wake-up call. Fortunately, and this is the genius of the book, McKenna not only awakens the reader to the vast potential of regional marketing, but he goes the extra mile of carefully revealing how to creatively think about the concept and its impact on the existing habits, practices, systems, and sacred cows of budgets, advertising, and promotion control.

Fortunately for the reader, McKenna goes far beyond simply laying out "how-to" guidelines and deals with the most fundamental issues of cultural diversity, customer alignment, multifunctional team building, and people empowerment. His counsel on understanding, managing, and connecting the human parts of the equation to the hard realities of the marketplace is an added value equally as important as the concept itself.

McKenna also keenly reminds us that access to information will replace access to capital as the key determinant for marketing success in the 21st century.

I will be very much surprised if this book doesn't become the official handbook for regional marketing development across the United States. To quote Francis Bacon, "If we are to achieve results never before accomplished, we must expect to employ methods never before attempted." McKenna takes you by the hand and leads you through those methods most of us have never attempted in exploring the rich opportunities afforded by regional marketing, a concept whose time has come.

LOU PRITCHETT
Retired Vice President, Worldwide Sales
The Procter & Gamble Company

When I was first asked to review this book, I was the vice president for Brand Marketing at Anheuser-Busch. I began the review process with a domestic business viewpoint in mind. About halfway through my review, I was made executive vice president of Marketing for Anheuser-Busch International. I now read the book for international benefit and application. After reviewing this book from two uniquely different perspectives, I believe it is the best work in the area of regional marketing that I have ever read. Additionally, this book goes far beyond regional marketing and offers points of view on management, sales, marketing, and training that are nuggets.

The strength of this book is its fundamental correctness. Shawn McKenna does not share proprietary information from his work experience or from his interviews. Instead, in a very sound and focused way, he pulls together information and points of view that have floated about on the subject for the last few years. His section on principles really forces you to challenge the way you currently conduct your marketing programs. Several aspects of the marketing mix are given detailed and poignant treatment. The section on understandings (the Marketing Assessment Process—MAP) formally unites all the things we marketers think we do, but probably don't.

As a marketer, this book spoke my language. The practical treatment of the sales and marketing topics in this book also makes it universally appealing to product and service businesses in most industries. Since regional marketing is thriving in overseas markets, this effort has broad international application as well. When I finally finished the manuscript, I spent some time reflecting on what I had read. My ultimate conclusion was that business people at all levels can certainly benefit greatly from this book. I wish this book had been available years ago.

JACK MACDONOUGH
Executive Vice President of Marketing
Anheuser-Busch International

I am delighted to have had the opportunity to read Shawn McKenna's *The Complete Guide to Regional Marketing*. The title is appropriate. It is, indeed, a complete guide to regional marketing. As such, it meets the needs of both practitioner and academician.

The author has managed to weave a fabric with the proper blend of theory and practice. That is, he relies on theory to explain why certain issues, analyses, and practices are necessary. He then segues quickly into an explanation of the practical steps that sound theory suggests must be accomplished to be successful. In short, it is an excellent blend of the why and how.

The author has also managed to achieve remarkable balance in the many examples he uses to illustrate key points. Industrial products and consumer goods and services examples literally pull the reader through each chapter. More extensive case illustrations are also included at several points.

Marketing professors will find a number of valuable uses for this book. All will want to convey the message contained in Section I—The Regional Marketing Imperative, Clash of Cultures, and Special Events: A Strategic Style. The book, however, will undoubtedly find its widest use as a companion piece to the traditional marketing management texts used in many undergraduate courses. It will prove especially helpful when dealing with the topic of market segmentation. At the graduate level and/or when dealing with case analysis, it will serve as a rich resource to illustrate good marketing practice in many of today's better-run companies. It permits the student to develop an idealized mental checklist of what to look for in both regional and national marketing programs.

In closing, this book should be kept within arm's reach of all marketing professors and their students.

JAMES F. ROBESON
Dean, School of Business Administration
University of Miami at Ohio

After having read Shawn McKenna's text on regional marketing, I am struck with the thought that this is potentially one of the most important books of any kind to be published in the United States this year. Why would I say this? Not just because it is an informative, educational, and easy-to-read treatise, all of which it certainly is, but because it has the potential to help us overcome one of the major plagues of U.S. business—the big company syndrome (or the loss of entrepreneurial spirit in corporate America).

As the chairman of an advertising agency that has worked with some of the largest companies and some of the smallest in the United States, I have had the opportunity to see the small guy win much more often than one would expect—a winning record I attribute to what I call an E-Brand or entrepreneurial brand mentality. This attitude assumes that a brand has no choice but to succeed. There is on the part of the management of these winning companies a sense of personal ownership (usually not literal) of the brand or brands they're marketing, a leanness in structure, and speed in decision making, all of which adds up to a greater chance for success in today's marketing environment.

I see regional marketing as a way for large U.S. corporations to get small, to promote an entrepreneurial spirit in their upcoming managers, to learn how to take risks (on a less-than-national level), and to promote a whole new spirit that leads *marketers* instead of accountants to the top of major corporations.

If the United States is ever to recover any of its past economic leadership, it will be because business management will have read and learned the lessons of books like Shawn McKenna's *The Complete Guide to Regional Marketing*, and hopefully taken to heart his call for the empowerment of regional managers. Through such empowerment mid-level U.S. management can learn again what made our industries great—the spirit of the E-Brand, the spirit of the entrepreneur.

WILLIAM G. TRAGOS
Worldwide Chairman and CEO
TBWA Advertising, Inc.

Preface

When this book was written, I was the Eastern Division Regional Marketing Manager for Procter & Gamble. In essence, this is a book on regional marketing done by a regional marketer.

I think this book will be very beneficial to any individual or business that is engaged or wants to be engaged in the discipline of regional marketing. However, this book goes far beyond my experience as a regional marketer. The value lies within the fact that the people I interviewed for the book developed the book's outline for me.

Within the past two years, I have spoken with over 100 people at all levels of business and education. My first question to them was this: "If you were to buy a book on the subject of regional marketing, what topics would need to be addressed to make you satisfied with your purchase?"

The three most common responses were as follows:

1. *Primarily, these people wanted to understand what principles to use to guide and/or develop regional marketing programs.* With that in mind, I developed Section 2, Regional Marketing Principles. This section deals with the general principles of being a regional marketer, the training a regional marketer needs, the way in which the position must be empowered, and the *right* support systems and

conditions to enable regional marketers to successfully do their job.

I have also developed principles for various marketing mix elements such as promotion, pricing, and advertising. I also discuss product packaging and distribution.

Author's note: I recognize that the key marketing mix elements are promotion, product, price, and place/distribution. Advertising is usually included within promotion, but I chose to treat advertising separately.

During the process of researching and writing this book, I discovered that these principles generally apply to most industries, from service companies to product companies. In essence, to understand the principles of regional marketing allowed me to journey confidently between industries.

2. *The next most frequently addressed topic was the area of assessment.* Specifically, people wanted to know when, where, and how to use regional marketing as a strategy in the marketplace.

In response, I developed Section 3, The Marketing Assessment Process (MAP)! This section deals with five primary understandings.

- Understanding your competition.
- Understanding your customer.
- Understanding your consumer.
- Understanding yourself.
- Understanding your turf.

I passionately believe that this section supersedes the topic of regional marketing and should be used to understand any business situation.

3. *The third most mentioned topic was identification of the right regional marketing style for a business.* Two of the most popular regional marketing styles today are special

events marketing and ethnic marketing. Many companies also believe that they practice regional marketing by having a micro-marketing focus. I somewhat disagree with this last statement and discuss this topic in Chapter 1.

Although I discuss special events marketing and ethnic marketing in some depth, I believe there are two *best styles* of regional marketing:

- *Regional Brand Strategies*. Wherein you develop a different regional approach for a particular brand. The approach may be different than the national strategy or complementary. In essence, you come to the conclusion that one size fits all marketing does not work for a particular brand in a particular regional marketplace.
- *"Customer-ized Marketing"*. (Recognize that I did not write *customized* marketing.) Customer-ized marketing treats each individual customer as the ultimate client.

This book is an example of customer-ized marketing. The responses of over 100 people interviewed profoundly adjusted the final product of this book and added dimensions that I had not originally planned to include. I listened and have humbly tried to deliver on behalf of their primary requests.

Thank you for buying this book. I hope that this work will meet or exceed your expectations. I would appreciate hearing from you with your thoughts on the book. Additionally, if you have any stories or points of view on regional marketing, please forward them to me. (If I use them in future books, I will give you credit for submission.) My address is as follows:

SHAWN MCKENNA
THE MCKENNA GROUP INTERNATIONAL
P.O. BOX 453
MANSFIELD, MASSACHUSETTS 02048

Acknowledgments

Although over 100 people contributed in some way to this book, I want to specially acknowledge 12 individuals:

- *Tom Quinn, President, Halperin Distributing Corporation.* Tom was "director of quality control" regarding this book. Tom took the special time to review each page with me. If I had contacted Tom sooner, undoubtedly I would have had him coauthor this book.

- *Scott Matthews.* Scott served as agent, marketer, and pre-editor. Scott helped me locate a publisher. After he helped secure an agreement with Business One Irwin, he helped edit the book and subsequently market it. Scott's early involvement gave me the confidence that my idea of a book on regional marketing could become a reality.

- *Anthony Morgan, Executive Vice President/Director of Strategic Planning, TBWA Advertising.* Tony was the one person whom I interviewed who did not *agree* with me as much as I would have liked. Tony provoked me to think more deeply about regional marketing than I had intended to. His good-natured and supportive critique of my work resulted in my writing a bit different book than I had planned.

- *Alex Wasilewski, Vice President, The Precept Group.* As a lifelong friend, Alex felt free to critique my book. Alex, like Tony, challenged me to take this book the "extra step "

My foreworders:

- *Mr. Lou Pritchett, Retired Vice President, Worldwide Sales, Procter & Gamble*
- *Mr. Jack MacDonough, Executive Vice President of Marketing, Anheuser-Busch International*
- *Dr. Jim Robeson, Dean, School of Business, University of Miami at Ohio*
- *Mr. Bill Tragos, Chairman/Chief Executive Officer, TBWA Advertising, Incorporated*

To all of you, a very warm "thanks" for reviewing my work and offering your support toward my effort. Reading the forewords that you provided gave me a tremendous sense of accomplishment and a verification that my effort was worthwhile.

- *Jeff Krames and Cindy Zigmund.* These were two of the finest senior editors a burgeoning author could have asked for. Jeff reviewed my initial book proposal and decided to take a chance on it. For that, I am eternally grateful. Cindy became involved once the book had been drafted and was supportive, professional, and brilliant with her contributions and insight.
- *Arden Roakes and Jeanette Casna.* Both Arden and Jeanette typed this book. Jeanette started the process and stopped to have a baby. (Congratulations!) Arden, who owns Pro To Type word processing, picked up where Jeanette left off and was also involved in pre-editing the book. My sincere thanks to both of you for meeting all the deadlines and not being too rough on the quality of my dictation.

Contents

SECTION I

Setting the Table

S ection I has three chapters. The first, entitled The Regional Marketing Imperative, discusses the benefits and development of regional marketing. I distinguish regional marketing from national mass marketing and briefly mention micro, target, and ethnic marketing and their relationship to a regional approach. I establish the idea that regional marketing is absolutely necessary for a company to successfully compete in today's business environment because many business categories have flattened out and matured. We just can't continue to squeeze more business out by doing the same efforts a little bit bigger every year. Regional marketing, if done well, can stimulate a new business awakening. I review a recent study by the Dechert-Hampe & Company, dealing with what companies think about regional marketing as we advance toward the year 2000.

Chapter 2 is a frank discussion of one of the true potential obstacles to successful regional marketing. When you regionally market, you often blend the sales and marketing disciplines. Historically, these departments in many companies have not blended well. If this issue of discipline integration is not remedied, the regional marketing function will be paralyzed.

Chapter 3 reviews a very popular regional marketing tactic called Special Events Management. Special events and local event marketing, while very important to regional marketing, are very specifically focused. In fact, since many people believe that local events are the epitome of regional marketing, I thought it appropriate to acknowledge this tactic's value early in the book.

Chapters 1 through 3 cover the topic, potential, and challenges of regional marketing. As the section title suggests these chapters serve to set the table for the three sections that follow: "Regional Marketing Principles," "Marketing Assessment Process" (MAP), and "Ultimate Regional Marketing."

Chapter One

The Regional Marketing Imperative

INTRODUCTION

Regional marketing, although not a new concept, is often a misunderstood term. I propose the following definition:

> Regional marketing: The process of dividing a company's general marketing area(s) into workable, well-defined geographic sections (markets). Regional strategies are then developed, and the marketing mix is flexed to service the needs and characteristics of the markets, customers, consumers, and company.

Simply stated, when you regionally market, you establish that the geographic variable is of primary importance, and all other aspects of marketing and sales are usually subordinate. Regional marketing is a macro-concept. Since the geographic region "reigns supreme," various styles of marketing integrate within the region at different times. The following chart (Figure 1–1) illustrates these marketing styles that periodically visit the individual marketing regions.

In Figure 1–1, regional marketing could easily be interchanged with national mass marketing. In fact, historically, the drawing of this starburst chart would be more accurate with national mass marketing as the center. However, today there is a wholesale swing to recognize the individual geographic regions with their panel of customers (trade channels) and consumers as

FIGURE 1–1
Marketing Types

the primary focus for most marketing and sales execution. The concept of "one size fits all" marketing, selling, and, to an extent, manufacturing and research and development are quickly fading. Although this book does not write the obituary for national marketing, it does reposition the regional variable as the primary concept for selling and marketing as we advance toward the 21st century.

As mentioned earlier, regional marketing is not a totally new concept. In fact, the service industry group and franchising phenomena have been profiting from regionally focused programming for quite some time. What is new, though, is that a vast majority of traditional marketers in such diverse industries as consumer pack-aged goods, airlines, automobiles, financial services, and others have been refocusing on the importance of regional marketing.

Today, more than ever, companies are taking a pluralistic approach to the way they do business. Traditional business norms are being set aside and wholesale paradoxical* shifts are taking place. One of the most important norms that has broken down is that national mass marketing is the only way. This has allowed regional marketing to emerge.

As recently as five years ago, it would have been heresy for companies such as Procter & Gamble, Nissan Motors, Merrill Lynch, and Metropolitan Life Insurance Company to deviate from their traditional national mass marketing style. However, these and other companies such as Campbell's, Anheuser-Busch, PepsiCo, Inc./Frito Lay, and The Coca-Cola Company have concluded that regional marketing can provide a valuable, competitive business edge.

The Dechert-Hampe & Company conducted a survey of manufacturing sales companies representing over $111 billion in sales. This survey, conducted in 1987, captured the growing importance of regional marketing and the developing shift away from national mass marketing. Figure 1–2 shows the dimension and timeliness of this regional marketing emer-gence. This chart evidences that fully 7 out of 10 companies have started to engage in regional marketing. The survey also forecasts that 9 out of 10 will be involved in regional marketing by the early 1990s.

REVOLUTION VERSUS EVOLUTION

Revolution happens quickly and usually recklessly and is bred by impatience and a need to react. Evolution takes more time and usually happens through proactive behavior. Regional marketing is a strong strategy that should mandate a degree of

---

* Paradoxical (paradox): a tenet contrary to received opinion.

FIGURE 1–2
The Emergence of Regional Marketing

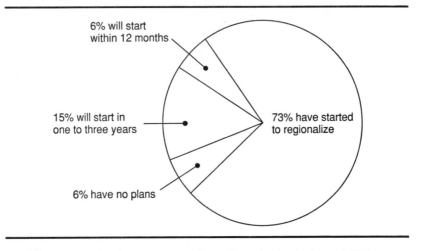

6% will start
within 12 months

15% will start in
one to three years

6% have no plans

73% have started
to regionalize

Source: Michael Raffini, "Regional Marketing: Survey Shows Accelerating Interest," *DHC Viewpoint* (Dechert-Hampe & Company, Winter 1987–88), pp. 1–2.

evolution. Evolution in a business sense does not have to take years. Instead, prudent and well planned change can happen comfortably within a year. Regional marketing should not be treated as a "flavor of the month"; it should be viewed as a strategy for the future.

Therefore it was surprising to find that very few companies surveyed seemed to be rolling out regional marketing by using any real test experience or by developing training programs. In fact, the same Dechert-Hampe survey revealed that a startling 7 out of 10 companies did not (at the time of survey) have regional marketing training programs in place. Please see Figure 1–3.

While conducting interviews and research for this book, I noticed that nearly 50 percent of the companies I reviewed had specific regional marketing training programs (50 companies were interviewed). However, upon reviewing the frameworks of these training programs, I discovered that only three of the companies had what I would consider legitimate programs. Additionally, none of the companies had programs targeted towards *full-service* regional marketing training within their respective industries.

FIGURE 1–3
Underwhelming Training Focus

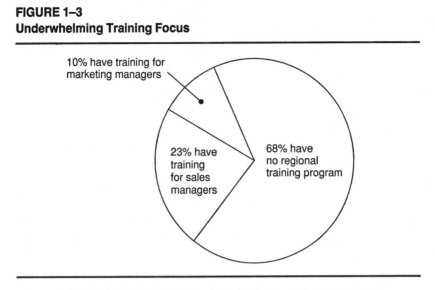

10% have training for
marketing managers

23% have
training
for sales
managers

68% have
no regional
training program

Source: Michael Raffini, "Regional Marketing: Survey Shows Accelerating Interest," *DHC Viewpoint* (Dechert-Hampe & Company, Winter 1987–88), pp. 1–2.

The implications of this new emergence and lack of training were substantiated by additional information obtained from the Dechert-Hampe survey.

Regional Marketing Funding Levels
(Information from companies with regional marketing programs in place)

- Forty-three percent said regional marketing programs will get 20 percent or less of the total marketing budgets in the coming year.
- Twenty-five percent put their commitment at 21 to 40 percent of the total marketing budget.
- Fully 18 percent said programs tailored to specific markets will get more than 40 percent of total marketing budget funding.[1]

---

[1] Michael Raffini, "Regional Marketing: Survey Shows Accelerating Interest," *DHC Viewpoint* (Dechert-Hampe & Company, Winter 1987–88), pp. 1–2.

It is easy to understand why I term the emergence of regional marketing in the late 1980s as a revolution in contrast to an evolution. As with most revolutions, there has been bloodshed. Many companies have misfired with their initial regional marketing efforts. Additionally, a revolution usually signals a change in strategy. Initially, the tactics don't quickly catch up with the strategy change unless someone spends strong initial effort to bring about strategic and tactical alignment. Even prototypical regional sales organizations such as Campbell's and Frito Lay recognize that it sometimes takes more time than planned before these new directions reap enhanced profit, revenue, and share. However, if regional marketing is set up correctly and executed by trained professionals, it will succeed.

GLOBALIZATION

Globalization is currently the business buzz word of the day. The globalization concept is the development of worldwide brands with the utilization of global technology, production, and research and development efficiencies. Although this concept appears frequently in corporate journals and annual reports, companies need to add to it the concept of glocal to achieve the profitable fulfillment of their globalized visions.

GLOCAL

Specifically, glocal is a combination of global and local. The glocal concept is the integration of sales, marketing, advertising and, to a lesser extent, manufacturing into this global vision. It is beneficial to take advantage of world brands, technology, and development as long as you continue to sell and market with the local consumer and customer base in mind in the areas of sales, marketing, product positioning, and packaging variations. Advertising is a real cross over variable here. Advertising, on one level, should stay broad and as global as is practical. On the other hand, advertising can be regionalized to complement the local sales and marketing effort.

This concept of glocal is important because regional marketing is not confined only to the United States. In fact, international marketing has been more regionally focused due to the fractured and complex cultures outside of the United States. While there are very significant differences among cultures within the United States, these differences are minimal in comparison to what exists worldwide. In other words, decades of national mass marketing have made the U.S. consumer and customer much more homogeneous than their counterparts from the collective rest of the world. To most established foreign companies, the U.S. market is becoming mature. In essence, there may not be (on the surface) a greater upside business return for their investment. The reason for this is that generally, U.S. and foreign companies have treated the U.S. market as a monolith. Companies that treat the different U.S. regions the same way as their foreign markets (with unique differences) are finding more gold "in them thar hills."

MARKETING IN THE SOVIET UNION

The concept of glocal came to life for me when, while writing this book, I was asked to join the board of directors of a U.S. company. This company was already engaged in a joint venture program with the Soviets and needed some help with sales and marketing. The company was marketing a global sports product. My first thought was that I didn't have significant international marketing experience; therefore, my value was to help advise with the domestic side of this company's business. However, once I traveled to the Soviet Union to work with our joint-venture partner, I quickly realized that to have a thorough understanding of regional marketing was to have a significant business edge internationally. In fact, as a result of that experience, I subtly adjusted some of the principles and concepts that are covered later in this book.

I am still involved with this venture and am convinced that the concept of glocal marketing is advanced by a thorough understanding of regional marketing. Regional marketing takes place all over the world.

NATIONAL TO REGIONAL: A NORMAL TRANSITION DUE TO INFORMATION

One of the primary reasons for the recent explosion in regional, targeted, segmented, micro, and specialized marketing is the exploding availability of information. Marketers know more about consumers and customers now than they did two or three years ago. In the consumer products business, there is almost more geo-demographic information available than mortals can synthesize, process, and make decisions from. In regional marketing, this knowledge means opportunity. The absence of knowledge, however, does explain why national mass marketing has been a preferred style for so long. Without information, you are tempted to sell and market to the largest possible audience your budget will allow. In a way, it is like panning for gold. You continue to sift until you find what you are looking for. Over time, the consumer and customer patterns that emerge add flavor and variation to national marketing programs.

While in the Soviet Union, I confirmed my belief that the availability of information is a primary contributor to the shifting from national to regional marketing. Basically, very little consumer or customer information is available there. In the absence of this information, traditional marketers are tempted to spend their budgets in the broadest way possible. I was not an exception, but my regional marketing background surely influenced my spending mix. My approach in the Soviet Union was to spend less than 25 percent of the dollars available in a mass marketing effort. The balance of the advertising dollars was spent to obtain information (as best as we could) from groups that seemed to be attracted to the particular product or service.

Some Regional Information Examples

Again, the availability and use of information are directly responsible for this marketing renaissance. Whether it be census information, customer service survey information, or retailer scanner information, regional information is available and can be utilized by regional managers and marketers. The following are some examples of a combination of a regional focus and regional information to gain business advantages:

- A savings and loan shows penetration of accounts by zip code and percentage of accounts per number of households in their marketing area.
- A leading life insurer measures actual sales versus market potential by country and zip code, in order to pinpoint where new agents are most needed. The company also measures its progress through its reaching equal opportunity hiring goals.
- A well-known direct marketer of outdoor clothing chooses drop points for deliveries of goods most convenient to its resources and its customers.
- A major regional utility compares demographic data with billing and consumption files to help chart energy conservation campaigns and forecast future power needs.[2]
- A large consumer goods company identifies large-size product opportunities based upon average household size and income and develops "heavied up" marketing programs in selected regions to sell large sizes.

---

[2] Thomas W. Osborn, "Analytic Techniques for . . . Opportunity Marketing," *Marketing Communications* (September 1987), p. 58.

Western Union Case Study

The following is a Western Union case study that will serve as a final example of how the attraction and possession of key regional marketing information has influenced one company's business.

> With labor and office costs skyrocketing, Western Union was looking for ways to preserve fine customer service in all of its markets, while maintaining the bottom line. The answer lay in replacing expensive Western Union offices with more cost-effective agencies, a mammoth micro-marketing problem. GSI/Tactics was a natural choice since it views micro-marketing as "the management of business on the basis of local profit potential."
>
> For Western Union, the micro-marketing strategy focused on a market-by-market evaluation of

the number of agents needed

where convenience for customers could be improved

where new market opportunities could be better served, and

where new agents could be profitably located.

The specific approach taken included:

determining the profile of the Western Union money-wire customer

identifying the geographic distribution of potential zip code level

matching current agent locations with potential to define zip areas as being

- unserved
- partially served
- saturated by existing agents

> The project involved the application of location modeling and optimization software provided by GSI/Tactics to evaluate the distribution of over 10,000 existing offices and agents, and help plan the location of several thousand new agencies. The resulting analyses gave every zip code in the country a demand and supply value and a demographic profile of the type of Western Union customer that could be expected to use wire services. In addition,

market area maps were produced to show the geographic distribution of

current business transactions

location of existing agencies

market potential for wire services

where to add new agents

As a result of this program, a significantly more efficient and cost-effective delivery system for the Western Union service was developed, resulting in increased market coverage and revenues. The matching of market area analysis to manager responsibility helped accelerate the implementation of the program by field managers. In addition, GSI/Tactics provided tactical management training, which brought the micro-marketing analysis and planning in-house. "GSI/Tactics helped teach our regional managers how to place agents geographically, so that they could continue the process on their own," notes Mel Harbinger, Senior Director of Market Research.[3]

PHASING INTO REGIONAL MARKETING

If the regional marketing focus is completely new for your company, it is unwise to rush into it. There is little disagreement that the concept of regional marketing is correct. However, there is much debate about the correct way to implement and execute this concept.

When introducing regional marketing, pay attention to these three areas: support systems, management layering and expense, and decentralized marketing.

SUPPORT SYSTEMS

A little later in the book, I will discuss whether or not the regional marketer should be located at the headquarters or in

---

[3] Ibid., pp. 58–59.

the field. The choice may seem obvious on paper, but in practice it was not that easy for me. For this discussion, let's assume the regional marketer is field based. On the front end of this transitional state, the field offices are probably the best and most logical host for the regional marketer. Support systems are in place that can be immediately accessed by regional marketers. Before this transition to the field, pay special attention to the particular marketing systems that may be needed to do the regional marketing job. There is often an absence of marketing research and statistical information in the field sales offices. Usually, this can be remedied by having the field office computers linked up with the central office network. Of course, field locations also need appropriate software packages in order to prevent regional marketers who come to the field with a high level of autonomy/ownership from having to trouble the central office for replenishment of their informational lifeline.

Secretarial/support staff as well as a copier, a fax, and some level of computer support should already exist in the regional sales offices, but this should *not* be assumed. Be sure to conduct a thorough fact-finding process to ensure that these new regional marketers do not begin their work with a handicap.

> *Author's note: If you do not have field sales offices, the job can be successfully administered out of a home office environment. Personally, I started in a field office setting and moved after a year to a home office.*

MANAGEMENT LAYERING AND EXPENSE

The second area of concern is directly related to the first. Specifically, when you add a regional marketing management tier, you are also adding a layer on top of an existing organization. I would recommend that before the regional marketing layer is introduced, the organization review its own methods and resources to see if there is possible excess capacity in the system regarding support staff and sales and marketing management. I believe that more than enough budget and staffing room should exist in an organization that has not restructured in the last two to three years. Look inwardly very carefully before you choose to expand the size of your organization. If staffing the regional marketing function can be a neutral to minimal incremental expense for the organization, then upper management will have patience with the development of this function. Otherwise, there may be extreme pressure for an immediate short-term payout to occur. When this happens, unnatural and unproductive behaviors take place that could ultimately lead to the abandonment at large of the regional marketing function.

DECENTRALIZED MARKETING

This third area will be covered in Chapter 2. The notion of decentralizing the marketing function is a very extreme one to marketers who have historically been tightly and centrally controlled.

Because of my experience with a strong centralized marketing approach, I do place a high premium on some form of central marketing organization. There should be a compromise between the totally decentralized organizations and the totally centralized one. There should be some centrally managed marketing programs so that there is continuity, consistency, and efficiency. Companies such as PepsiCo, Inc. do this very well because they often conduct corporate promotions that the regional bottlers customize for their markets. Additionally, the regional bottlers have a budget from which they can collectively, say, in groups of five to eight bottlers within the region, run their own locally targeted promotion. This promotion has to be consistent with some of the general corporate strategies but is totally owned and managed by the local organization.

Again, the phenomenon of decentralized marketing should be recognized as a concern. Not all concerns are opportunities; however, once an organization finds a comfortable balance between the centralized and decentralized approach, then regional marketing magic occurs.

TRANSITION STATE

Phase One: Regional Management

Before you introduce regional marketing, it is essential that you feel comfortable with your regional sales management and support structure in the field. If these vital "anchors" are not reasonably capable, introducing a new element to the mix (regional marketing) could hurt both. Regional marketing could become frustrated, and regional management (sales) could feel threatened. Above all else, be confident with your regional sales organization before you introduce the regional marketing function.

Phase Two: Test Drive

Procter & Gamble has been criticized for its desire to test market almost every new product it introduces. Critics indicate that test marketing reveals your national plan to the competition. The introduction of regional marketing to an area is like a new product introduction; however, the product is hardly top secret. Competition can be generally aware that you are introducing regional marketing into your overall sales and marketing mix, but it would be very hard for them to find specific strategic and operational details. On the other hand, when you introduce a new cookie, you can bring back the packaging, the product, and introductory sales materials to analyze. Additionally, you can turn on the television to see what kind of copy choices the company is making behind this new brand effort.

Testing a regional marketing structure is very prudent and can debug your process. Don't be shy about overstaffing your test market. My intention is not for you to have better than national hypothetical results. On the contrary, I hope that you can develop additional people in the process so that they can be deployed to other regions. They would already have some practical experience and could help set up and lead those regional marketing organizations.

Phase Three: Integration of Regional Marketing into the Marketing Mix Elements

Do not simultaneously introduce regional marketing efforts within the marketing mix items of promotion, pricing, advertising, and product. You should sequence your regional marketing application subject to the type of industry that you are in. Generally, I would recommend the following approach for most business categories:

1. *Promotion*
It is assumed in the two previous phases that these new regional marketers are well trained. I will discuss this in detail in Chapter 4. If these people are well trained and recruited, you must give them something to do immediately upon their being chartered. Promotion is the first marketing mix element that regional marketers ought to use. The area of promotion is alive and does not usually have much downside risk associated with it. Some people probably disagree with that statement. However, the risk associated with promotion is proportionally smaller than errors with regional pricing, regional product choice, or regional advertising. Promotion usually affects a smaller group of consumers and can be financially controlled based upon the number of events deployed.

Since I recommend that central brand organizations still conduct relevant national promotions, this provides a good opportunity for regional marketers to work with the central marketing organization. The first phase ought to be taking the national promotion and customizing or regionalizing it to the local market. Once that takes place, regional marketers should then test some of their own local promotions with a careful eye to the national promotion calendar and the national and/or regional brand strategy. Close alignment is important as regional marketing is "powered up." Once consistent alignment takes place and the quality of the programs is achieved, there will be a higher confidence level between the central marketing organization and the regional marketers.

A special note on promotion: **Any new program needs a few initial good wins.** Make sure your first regional promotional executions are simple, easy to measure, and deliver good results. Avoid overly complicated initial programs. It is important not to embarrass the function or to fail at the outset.

2. Pricing

Maintain a strong adherence to national pricing on products wherever possible. This varies incredibly by industry and, in some cases, pricing is generally the same for a product or service by all competition within a region.

In Chapter 6, I state that, in at least the consumer packaged goods business, there should always be a central pricing coordinator. To decentralize the pricing function in this industry could create chaos or regional marketing mania. It is not practical or strategic for regional marketers and sellers to be kept out of the regional pricing equation. This is very important when regional brand strategies are developed. Regional pricing, when it comes to an integrated regional brand strategy, cannot be segregated from the promotion, product, and advertising variables.

Since regional pricing has high risk, specific training should be a prerequisite. Pricing, especially regional, needs the appropriate checks and balances. Only a central pricing coordinator can ensure this.

3. Product

Many companies have been introducing products regionally for quite some time. I put product third in sequence because I would want regional marketers to gain a better overall understanding of the business via promotion and pricing before researching and then recommending regional product decisions. Once a regional product decision has been made and the various manufacturing, distribution, advertising, and research and development organizations have signed off, then the entry of this regional product should be fairly normal for both the sales and marketing organization to handle.

4. Advertising

The views that I share in this book *generally* reflect a constituency approach to writing. By that, I mean that if I interviewed 20 people on special events marketing and 15 made a specific point, then I usually expressed that point in the book. Thus, my views reflect a reasonably well-balanced consensus.

With advertising as the fourth integrated element of the marketing mix, I violate the consensus principle and override my interviewees. In fact, I had very little agreement that this should be sequentially last. Most people indicated that it would be very easy to execute regional advertising subject to executing local television buys versus national in some markets. Additionally, they indicated that it wouldn't be much trouble to customize items such as billboards, radio, and print. While my concern usually is the execution of regional marketing, in this case, the need was for the delicate treatment of advertising.

Many companies do both regional and national advertising. But when you transfer from a truly national advertising (principally television) approach to a regional approach with possibly different copy and media variations, this transition should be given time. Since advertising reaches such a broad, large audience, the risk of fielding non-strategic advertising to a region is high. I am not talking about running national copy with a five-second tag on the end that regionalizes this copy. This strategy could be a fine first step and could happen almost at once. My caution, and thus my prioritizing this marketing mix element last, is directed more toward a high-quality, very segmented advertising approach.

Chickens and Eggs

Views about regional marketing can be illustrated by the classic breakfast analogy about the pig and the chicken making their mutual offering to the traditional breakfast of bacon and eggs. The chicken makes a contribution to breakfast by providing the egg, but the pig makes a supreme commitment by providing the bacon. Companies (no disrespect intended) are pigs or chickens when it comes to regional marketing. Some do not feel comfortable making the supreme commitment to a regional marketing philosophy, principally because of a lack of knowledge and/or a belief that regional marketing is right for their business. Other companies have moved forward wholeheartedly (Campbell's, Nissan Motors, and Frito Lay). Since regional marketing is here to stay as a very important way of doing business, companies need to consciously recognize the tremendous opportunity that regional marketing presents.

Regional marketing is probably the singular best way to align with both our business customers and the ultimate consumer. Clearly, there is some risk, but there can be greater reward.

Ownership versus Custodial

Moving to a total regional marketing point of view, or at least a combined regional/central marketing position, really unleashes the secret weapon in people and organizations—ownership! Businesses need to find ways to move people from custodial relationships to ownership relationships. Ownership refers to an attitude versus an equity relationship. Ownership exists when people feel empowered and when people believe they are responsible for the creation, implementation, and execution of programs. This ownership translates to a high degree of pride and involvement, which benefits the organization in all aspects.

R.O.E.

Regional marketing, more than any form of marketing, unleashes what I call R.O.E.! This stands for Return on Employee! Most of us have traditionally been preoccupied by R.O.I.—Return on Investment and R.O.N.A.—Return on Net Assets. Regional marketing makes owners out of our future upper managers, and it develops an intrepreneurial spirit that does not usually exist in central organizations or regional committees.

SUMMARY

Chapter 1 discusses my favoring a combined approach of regional marketing and centralized marketing. Companies have been centrally marketing for decades, and I hope that this book will coach you on how to harness the untapped potential of regional marketing. Regional marketing can either be a solid adjunct strategy or general replacement strategy to the way you market today. This chapter has been titled the Regional Marketing Imperative. Imperative means that regional marketing is necessary. Its call cannot be ignored.

Companies involved with regional marketing need to give it time. If executed correctly, a regional marketing program will return near and long-term dividends. For companies flirting with regional marketing the time has come to try it because if you don't deploy this strategic edge, you can rest assured that your competition will.

SUMMARY CHECKLIST

1. *Does a "one size fits all" marketing strategy really work for your product?*

2. *Is your company embarking on a real or pseudo regional marketing program without properly training its people? Are your people really trained well enough to manage the investment of regional marketing funds?*

3. *Is your strategy changing so quickly that your tactics are having trouble catching up?*

4. *Is your company so "starry eyed" about globalization that the logic of regional sales, marketing and advertising linkage is missing? (Glocal)*

5. *Do you have the right support systems in place to sustain regional marketing? Do you have good regional business information?*

6. *Before you "staff up" for regional marketing, have you looked towards reasonable consolidation to avoid increased management layering and expense?*

7. *Have you planned carefully to avoid conflict between regional and national efforts? (Don't totally decentralize.)*

8. *Are you planning on phasing into regional marketing or jumping into regional marketing?*

9. *Can you really create an ownership attitude versus a custodial one?*

Chapter Two

Clash of Cultures

INTRODUCTION

For regional marketing to achieve its fullest potential, managers must guard against a conflict between the sales and marketing disciplines.

Regional marketing, by its very nature, leads to a *level* of decentralized marketing, which is discussed later in the book. However, a balance between centralized and decentralized efforts is needed. Specifically, regional marketing should complement central marketing. Regrettably, many organizations have plunged headfirst into regional marketing without recognizing the consequences this process potentially has with in-place people and systems.

A clash between marketing and sales is very predictable because regional marketing is a level where they operationally both come together. This convergence is more than a short-term visit. Instead, it is an ongoing process. Sellers and marketers often interact in the normal course of business through new item initiatives, promotion plan orientation, and other areas of sales and marketing planning. However, these contacts are usually linear relationships. By that, I mean marketers recognize opportunity and develop products and programs to meet that opportunity. Sellers then take the programs and implement them on behalf of the company. Sometimes, sellers give feedback to marketers about the successes and failures of the programs. When this occurs, an

informational loop takes place, and sometimes the relationships are prolonged for perceived mutual benefit. However,
these relationships usually exist from program to program
instead of being an ongoing interrelated process. The differences between the two organizations, while often appropriate in the traditional sales and brand structure, must be
managed to avoid a counterproductive relationship.

CULTURAL DIVERSITY

I have received extensive training in the area of valuing cultural
diversity. This training, which focused on ethnicity, religious
beliefs, age, and gender, has been fairly traditional and straightforward. What I propose here is for companies to expand their
diversity training to go even deeper than these previously mentioned areas. Functional departments within companies also
have similar cultural relationship problems. Therefore, when
dealing with the departments of finance, research and development, manufacturing, sales, and marketing, we should use the
same approach we would use if we were dealing with the integration of Hispanics, Asians, blacks, and whites.

To advance our mutual interests, we first need to seek an
understanding of the different departmental cultures and then
recognize the importance of valuing cultural differences.

An Understanding

Although it is important to gain a specific understanding of the
different multifunctional groups, for regional marketing, it is
important to focus in the first phase on the differences and
points in common between sellers and marketers. To do this, I
spoke to a wide range of people from both disciplines and from
different types of companies. Interestingly, the responses from
people in large companies, small companies, for-profit organizations, and nonprofit organizations were similar. Table 2–1
summarizes the most commonly used descriptions offered by

sellers and marketers about themselves and their counterparts. The table should clearly identify that while there are some points in common there are many points of distinction.

TABLE 2–1
Perceptions

How Salespeople Describe Themselves	How Marketers Describe Salespeople
1. Volume-oriented	1. People-oriented
2. People managers	2. People managers
3. Nonpolitical	3. Short-sighted
4. Aggressive/doers	4. Good verbal communicators
5. Intuitive/instinctive	5. Nonstrategic thinkers
6. Fun-loving	6. Frustrated with bureaucracy
7. Committed to their work	7. Arrogant
8. Less analytical	8. Implementers
9. Independent	9. Older/more career-oriented
10. Long-termers	10. "Good old boy" networkers

How Marketers Describe Themselves	How Salespeople Describe Marketers
1. Aggressive	1. Good project managers
2. Strategists	2. Less experienced/younger
3. Diverse	3. Politically motivated
4. Analytical	4. Arrogant
5. Leaders	5. Data-oriented/analytical
6. Highly competitive	6. Volume blind/profit share-oriented
7. Profit-motivated	7. Well educated
8. Share-driven	8. Non risk takers
9. Project/program specialists	9. Less instinctive
10. In charge	10. Short-termers

CORPORATE SPEAK

To further complicate this situation, each department (somewhat like different branches of the armed service) has its own "corporate speak" internal language. This became very apparent to me when I attended my first multidisciplined core team meeting. Our team was established to help shepherd a new product initiative through to completion. This team had representatives from finance, research and development, product supply/manufacturing, advertising, and sales. One member of the team discussed the subject of payout. I represented sales, and my definition of payout was different than the speaker's definition. I interrupted the discussion and asked the other team members what they thought the term *payout* meant. Amazingly, none of us at the meeting had exactly the same definition and understanding of payout. Bringing this discord to people's attention forced us to backtrack because two other expressions (manufacturing terms) used earlier in the meeting were unfamiliar to a few people in the room. From that point on, we tried to keep our departmental jargon to a minimum and talk in a common language. In Chapter 11, I discuss the notion of corporate language and its importance.

MISINTERPRETATIONS ABOUND

Desmond Morris in *Manwatching* points out that one familiar gesture, the circle made with thumb and forefinger, may have totally different meanings in different cultures and contexts.

Possible meanings:

A-OK; everything's fine; perfect. (USA, UK, much of Europe)

He's a zero; don't pay any attention to him; don't take him seriously. (France)

An obscene characterization of a third person, or an obscene accusation. (Certain Mediterranean countries)

Please give me change (coins). (Japan)[1]

I spoke with Tom Quinn, President of Halperin Distributing Corporation, about the differences between sellers and marketers. Tom was experienced in both marketing and sales because he worked in both disciplines with Procter & Gamble before he accepted his current position. Tom best summed up the difference between sales and marketing with the following analogy.

> The difference between sales and marketing really can be described best by reviewing the selection process of the starting pitcher for the World Series. A marketer would spend days in intensive meetings and analysis to determine who would have the probability of pitching the best during game one. Marketers would struggle with all kinds of data and do several types of statistical modeling. Once they made their decision, they would transmit that to the salespeople and then barely look back. In fact, they would commence almost immediately to figure out through the same process to decide who should pitch game two. A salesperson, on the other hand, would choose the pitcher who was "hot" and not really care about the process of selection. The seller also wouldn't even be thinking about the second game's starting pitcher until the first game was completed.

Managing the differences between sellers and marketers makes everyone's life a little bit happier. To proactively manage this conflict to benefit regional marketing, the following tactical steps should be taken:

1. *Enrollment.* Have upper management (either general, sales, or marketing) communicate the interim and long-term value of the regional marketing position. This will enroll the primary disciplines and encourage acceptance.

---

[1] Dr. George Simms, "Section Three—Manage the Unspoken—Gestures," *Working Together* (Los Altos, Calif.: Crisp Publication, Inc., 1989), p. 46.

2. *Co-design.* Have a small group of sellers and marketers (together) develop the framework of regional marketing for your company.

3. *One overall leader.* Ensure that one person's job is to lead the design process and ensure that the design is communicated and implemented.

4. *Systems and principles.* Make sure that adequate systems are in place and that principles and procedures have been developed to guide the areas of operation. Additionally, make sure there is consensus between sales and marketing regarding recruitment, training, status, and reporting lines of individuals.

5. *"On-boarding".* Ensure that the new regional marketing managers understand that the failure of the sales and brand organization to interrelate effectively at the regional marketing level is a dangerous virus. Ideally, it would be nice if the members of the design group were to become the eventual regional marketing managers.

6. *Audience awareness.* Make sure the various audiences in your company are comfortable with the knowledge about regional marketing and how it will be deployed. This is important so that other affiliated disciplines and groups within your organization are made to feel important by this information sharing. I recommend that these groups not be communicated to all at once in a large room. Instead, it is appropriate for the overall regional marketing leader to visit one-on-one with the leaders of the various departments and organizations with which regional marketing will interact.

7. *Managing culture as an ongoing process.* Because cultures evolve and people-turnover exists, there should be an automatic commitment to maintaining a healthy cultural environment. I spent a great deal of time when I first became a regional marketing manager bonding with the other regional marketing managers and doing personal orientation with other department personnel. However, within the first two years of our regional marketing test, all of the regional marketing managers had left except for me. Further, 80 percent of the brand managers with whom I had dealt two years earlier had either been promoted or left the company. Over time, I began running into the cultural difference problems when interacting with new sales managers and marketing managers. What I had failed to do was to take responsibility for orienting these new internal customers as they assumed their new positions. To manage this better, the regional marketing function became a mandatory item within the framework of new-manager orientation. Once every three months or so, I spoke with a group of five to ten new managers. This flexible, small-group environment helped me to work with these new managers, and I was also periodically revitalized by their enthusiasm.

8. *Multidiscipline cross-training.* Encourage whenever possible that ongoing training programs be multidepartmental (functionally diverse). Interacting with the other disciplines on subjects common to all of us (like basic skill training) really helps broaden our overall understanding and builds mutual respect between the departments.

9. *Having fun.* This is not so much a step as an attitude. It is important to invest in relationships. It is very obvious that this investment should be business and pleasure. As Table 2A, which describes sellers' and marketers' opinions of each other, indicates, we need to improve. Having fun is a universal bridge over communication gaps. However, the fun should not be at the expense of others but should be in concert with others. Jeff Prouty, the principal of the Prouty Project, believes in fun with a twist. Mr. Prouty's company is an adventure-based, team-building company in Minneapolis, Minnesota. Mr. Prouty indicates that "having fun, yet also being challenged, is perhaps the ultimate state of team building. You should also not overlook the fact that, while it is obvious that different disciplines need to be helped to relate, there are also wide gaps within individual disciplines."

I can speak firsthand that fun, challenging, out-of-character-type team activities go amazingly far in overcoming corporate cultural chasms. When I initially became involved with a business category, the general manager organized a day-long war game for all of us. This activity brought all the disciplines together, and then we worked as teams. This activity worked extremely well because everybody participated. However, we need to avoid setting up fun programs that are offensive to people or physically prohibitive.

The nine tactical steps just mentioned will aid the cultural blending process significantly. However, to break down the issue of departmental cultural clashes takes more than that. Specifically, there is a real need to focus on three key areas:

1. *Organization/department preconditions.* In Chapter 11, I deal with this issue in detail. Organizational preconditions are statements in the area of vision, mission, values, and principles. If you want to understand and work compatibly with an organization, it is critical to have a comfortable understanding of these four preconditions. Too often, the sales and marketing functions have no idea about the feelings of each individual department in these four areas. If we truly believe that we are on the same team, then it should be mandatory (especially when engaging in regional marketing) to understand your and your partner disciplines' preconditions. You then will probably want to align your regional marketing function within these preconditions wherever possible.

2. *Understand each other's organizational roots.* Specifically, understand how the people in each function have been recruited. Did each organization go through the same interview process? If not, then what were the specific areas of distinction within the process? If you know the difference in the interview focuses, then you can quickly understand the people differences within the respective departments.

Beyond recruiting, you need to understand how each organization has been trained. What is stressed? What is left out? Most importantly, you need to know how each organization measures performance and rewards its individuals. These areas are important not only to coexist functionally within the regional marketing framework but also to design a productive and cohesive regional marketing work unit. Pull together the valuable parts of each individual training and management program as a starting point for regional marketing training. Then, as you understand the needs of regional marketing better, try to merge these programs into your own composite training programs. A general regional marketing training outline is shared in Chapter Four.

3. *Understand each department's norms, procedures, and rules.* It is very important to identify these items early in the team-building relationship. If you are procedurally blind relative to the needs and constraints of each organization, all your best ideas could be superseded by the need for procedural obedience.

These three focuses should be given emphasis and must be addressed during the co-design phase not only of managing this clash of cultures but also in developing the regional marketing program.

Organizational loyalty is a strong factor. Don't be discouraged if, as you bring up your new regional marketing team, most people live for varying amounts of time in the past. I have gone through many transitions in my career and find that it usually takes me between two and three months to change my vernacular from *they* to *we* in describing my new organization.

SUMMARY

I had a wonderful experience becoming involved from the ground up with regional marketing at Procter & Gamble. However, one of the most uncomfortable parts of an otherwise pleasant process came in the area of this clash of cultures. It is initially difficult for people to master the art of speaking two languages (sales and marketing). I recall one particular example. I had spent a lot of time working on a "bed and breakfast" program for one of our brands. From a purely sales perspective, I did not think that this would be a huge volume opportunity, but it was strategically right for the brand. Local sales management did agree to become somewhat involved and support it with a reasonable effort. Then, I also worked with an assistant brand manager and the advertising agency to develop a total marketing, advertising, and sales plan. I accepted this project because it seemed easy to execute from a sales point of view, it identified well with the regions I managed, and it supported the brand's overall strategy. Once I pulled the plan together, I got sales management's concurrence and then scheduled what I thought would be an automatic meeting with the brand manager. At that meeting, I quickly realized I had misread the marketing culture. I will, however, admit that the assistant brand manager should have managed this issue for me. About a quarter of the way through my presentation, the brand manager indicated that the project was valueless and it was a waste of time for us to be spending our resources in such an unproductive way. Upon further questioning, I learned that the brand manager really did like the program; however, timing and conditions were all wrong. I should have known, after having worked on the brand, that this request was going to be in trouble. First of all, I was requesting money *after* the budget had been finalized, so I was asking for money from a very small reserve balance. Additionally, the brand was having significant volume shortfalls and was under extreme pressure to deliver on its profit commitment. This combination of business circumstances and poor timing was a fundamental mistake on my part because I had forgotten my knowledge of the marketing culture. I never made that mistake again!

Corporate and individual cultural difference is great. The key to unleashing this difference to enrich organizations and individuals is to understand both the whats and whys. Whats are the actions, and whys are the reasons. If a member of a group is behaving (from *your* perspective) counterproductively, find out why. The whys are usually more important than the whats. An example I frequently use is getting slapped on the back of the head. That act (the what) is a hostile act. I did this to a good friend once with no warning. He immediately turned around and responded with a series of unpleasantries. Imagine how embarrassed he felt when I showed him the dead wasp that I had hit and knocked off his collar. I could not warn him because I knew he was terrified of wasps. While the *what* (the hit) was extreme, the *why* (the wasp) was much more important. We all need to better understand the whys.

SUMMARY CHECKLIST

1. *Do you understand the vision, mission, values, and principles of the organization you are partnering or working with?*
2. *Are you aware of the profile of the other organization's people? Do you know this organization's recruiting, training, measurement, and reward systems?*
3. *Are you comfortable with understanding the norms, habits, traditions, procedures, rules, and constraints of the other organization?*
4. *When designing regional marketing, will you have representatives from both the selling and marketing disciplines actively participate?*

   Author's note: This is not only important for the compatibility of the team/regional marketing members, but is also important for understanding how to interrelate with the two different disciplines.

5. *Has upper management blessed the chartering of regional marketing?*
6. *Do you have one overall leader (owner) of both the design process and the merchandising of the function to the other disciplines?*
7. *Are appropriate systems and operating principles in place to attend to the different multifunctional needs?*
8. *Do your people strongly identify with the notion that sales and marketing relationship problems can severely hurt regional marketing?*
9. *Have you intimately spoken with different multifunctional disciplines that will interrelate with regional marketing?*
10. *Does your organization understand that managing culture is an ongoing and evolving process? Do you appreciate the differences between whats and whys?*

11. *Do you encourage multidiscipline cross-training?*

12. *Do you plan to continually bring new participants into the process?*

13. *Is your organization truly committed to moving the business ahead and committed to having fun?*

Author's note: Don't misinterpret this point to be a casting call for organizational comedians. However, if you can have people believe that their work is sincerely fun, then the atmosphere, attitude, and results will be high performance.

Chapter Three

Special Events: A Strategic Style

INTRODUCTION

Regional marketing as a broad topic takes several specific shapes. While there are literally scores of different ways you can regionally market, there are four primary styles:

1. Special events marketing.
2. Ethnic targeted marketing.
3. Regional brand strategies.
4. Customer-ized marketing.

This chapter deals primarily with the first style, special events marketing. Style two will be covered in Chapter 10. Regional brand strategies and customer-ized marketing will be reviewed in great length in Chapters 11 and 12.

The special events marketing business is growing at a rapid pace, both domestically and internationally. Special events marketing has now become a multibillion dollar business with hundreds of companies vying for available special events marketing funds.

Special events take many shapes and sizes and are dominated by sporting, concert, and community-type programs. One need only subscribe to *Special Events Report*, (213 West Institute Place, Suite 303, Chicago, IL 60610, telephone: 312-944-1727) published biweekly by International Events Group, to understand just what kind of volume and variety exists in the special events business today.

The special events world is totally expandable because nearly everything is for sale or for sponsor. The special events sponsorship business, especially in sports marketing, has become incredibly competitive. Although there are hundreds of special events companies, the sports marketing field is dominated by "the big three" (International Management Group-IMG, ProServe, and Advantage International). In fact, special events warfare is getting so extreme that at least two of these three companies (at this writing) are actually buying some of the special event properties that they have been working with.

SPECIAL EVENTS ARE A REGIONAL MARKETING WEAPON

Special events as a style (tool) is very important to regional marketing as a concept. Companies use special events/local events within their marketing menu in varying degrees. Some companies, both large and small, participate only in a few special event programs. On the other hand some companies, like Anheuser-Busch, take special events marketing so seriously that they have their own in-house operation that can rival some of the best special events marketing companies in the world, both in terms of strategy and execution. Regardless of the dimension of involvement by companies in special events, one basic truth exists: special events done well can provide a regional competitive edge. Most often by the very nature of special events, the programs are regionally restricted. However, when you string together a network of special events, such as the Barnum & Bailey Circus tour (the circus visits over 90 cities across the United States annually), you have a program that is national.

Special events commingle very well with regional marketing and can be tactically correct for marketing within a region.

Special events have the potential to excel because of four basic reasons:

1. Special Events Are Generally Unduplicated by Competition

When you are regionally marketing behind a local special event (food festival, sporting event, cultural event), you generally, during the time of the event, have marketing category exclusivity. Companies usually demand exclusive rights for the event as a condition of sponsorship in order to block competitor participation. This is a standard operating procedure in local/special event promotional negotiation and is a significant feature for a company. Further, similar type events are rarely repeated soon after execution (except in professional sports).

2. Special Event Promotions Are Usually Nonprice-Related Events

While your product is associated with the local event, you generally don't have to deeply discount it (reduce the cost) to help sell your product. The association with the event and the advertising exposure that special events bring usually negates the short-term need of reducing the price of the product. In fact, if a company chooses to use a special event tactic for a product and concurrently deeply reduces the product cost during the special event, then the special event itself should be reviewed. The event and discounting are really a double expense to market the product and could be, after final analysis, cost prohibitive.

Price marketing, as will be mentioned in following chapters, usually is a short-term way to enhance sales. While discount pricing is a regional/national tactic, it should be a subordinate choice compared with other options. Companies should, however, gravitate toward long-term business-building programs in lieu of short-term pricing programs whenever they can. Special events usually provide just such a forum.

3. The Assimilation Factor

Local special events which already have built-in equity with local customers and consumers can help products gain acceptance within a market. If the local event is well done and positively received by the marketing area's consumers, then a product association with this event can really break down consumer barriers and help brands with trial, retrial, and continuity of purchase promotional strategies.

I witnessed this phenomenon take place during the summer of 1989 behind a Pringles corn crisp new product introduction. The Syracuse sales district had a positive experience by tying in with an unlimited hydroplane race at a lake near Syracuse, an event attended by several thousand people. Local supermarkets and other businesses promote the merchandise heavily with the hydroplane theme when the unlimited hydroplane tour stops in the Syracuse area.

Pringles sponsored an unlimited hydroplane boat named *Mr. Pringles*, which was used to stimulate trade and consumer interest in Pringles. The local sales management group, in conjunction with the Pringles brand, used the existing hydroplane special event to help introduce the new Pringles corn crisp flavors. In essence, the sales and brand team hooked these new flavors of Pringles into an already well-received (by the community and customer base) special event and were regionally very successful.

Several other marketing factors did come in to play, but the net result was that the Syracuse market had some of the highest share results of any market in the country, both during the special event and for a prolonged period after it.

4. Special Events Can Be Fun for Sellers and Buyers

The phrase "special event," by definition, suggests an activity that is usually fun and intriguing. Buyers and sellers often get bored with the routine of coupons, newspaper advertising, radio advertising, and television and are always looking for something different and exciting. Additionally, consumers are somewhat hypnotized by homogeneous marketing campaigns, which creates boredom and clutter in their minds space.

Generally, special events, if well planned and executed, are fun and rewarding for everyone they touch. When you have a happy relationship between the buying and selling function, you almost always will enjoy strong business results behind your program. Involvement with special events quite frequently is the high point of a seller's sales year. Because the seller is so enamored with this style of marketing, you frequently witness Herculean sales and marketing efforts as a result.

PROACTIVELY MANAGE SPECIAL EVENTS

As with any marketing approach or style, there are certain issues that have to be recognized. With special events, there are three primary issues that should be proactively addressed.

1. Try to Uncomplicate Special Events
In Chapter 5 I critically review a specific special event proposal. Needless to say, the example had so many frills that the event was not approved because of sheer complexity.

There is a tendency with special event programs to make them much more involved than they really need to be. My counsel would be to brainstorm on the 10 most important aspects of a special event and then do three or four of them very well. If you take my counsel a step further, you would probably find that I wouldn't be disappointed if you didn't even execute or become involved with the other six features. A good friend of mine who is an international sales manager with Procter & Gamble once said to me, "To do everything is to do nothing." When it comes to special events (especially in the first or second year of involvement), you can hinder your execution and business results by trying to do too much.

2. Don't Forget What Your Job Is
Very few companies have special events as one of their primary business approaches. Some notable exceptions (and rightfully so), like Anheuser-Busch, have such an impact on their consumers, their channel of distribution, and their brand image that special events marketing is a way of life. I agree with this strategy for Anheuser-Busch and its Budweiser brands, but I don't generally believe that most companies can mimic Anheuser-Busch's execution.

When a sales and marketing force loses focus of the primary purpose of the special event, the event itself is placed in jeopardy. Often sellers and marketers lose track of the initial objectives of a special event. When this happens, usually it is the beginning of the end. This experience, regrettably, is also very predictable, yet companies don't do much to proactively manage this lack-of-focus slump.

Lack of focus on the true objectives of the event happens by about year two or three of a program. Year one and *sometimes* year two usually benefit from the excitement, novelty, and momentum of the special event. Certainly, sales and marketing managers need to keep their eye on the business target with more intensity by about year three.

3. Special Events Can Be Cost-Prohibitive

During a review of special events principles later on in the chapter, I will discuss cost as it relates to profitability. However, the cost factor of special events is a significant issue. If a special event is a single event (versus involvement with, as mentioned previously, a 90-city Barnum & Bailey Circus), then the sheer economics of one-of-a-kind marketing may be very obstructive. It is important to emphasize *may be*! Managers who are not fans of special events will usually drift to this issue quickly with an I-told-you-so attitude. Be careful about this negative approach, because one-of-a-kind events can be very powerful for a market and, over time, can become very strong and profitable to the company. When it comes to cost, it is important to have a healthy and compromising attitude so that good ideas don't get dismissed because of some people's special events paradigms.

TEN SPECIAL EVENTS PRINCIPLES

I have been involved with special event management for several years and have evolved from a position of heavy cynicism to healthy respect for the benefits that special/local event programs can bring to a sales and marketing effort. My maturing on this subject has a direct correlation to my evolutionary belief in several special event principles. When I was cynical about special events, I fell into the camp of many non-planners and operated under the credo of "ready, fire, aim"! With the introduction and development of principles and then the subsequent adherence to those principles, I have now become a member of the "ready, aim, fire" club, which works much better. I just wish it hadn't taken me so long to treat special events more seriously and less like a hobby.

The principles that have helped me better understand and manage special events are as follows.

1. Sales and Marketing Expectations Must Be Clear, Derived from Consensus, Well Discussed before the Fact, and in Writing

The toughest management task with any program is usually the management of people's expectations. The litmus test for that comment really manifests itself in special events management. For this book, I interviewed many special events managers both from the product and agency side. Almost all of them cited a need to align expectations between the client and customer as vital. This is not only important from a conceptual point of view but also from an ethical, contractual, and sales and marketing execution framework as well. When developing these expectations, it is important to identify who is the financier in this relationship. Did the money to fund this program come from the sales organization or the marketing organization? Knowing who the financier is can be critical if there is to be a continuous history for this special event program.

A classic confrontation occurs in the special events arena when one organization emphasizes the trade-relationship-building elements of hospitality (typically, local sales management), and another organization (typically, central sales and marketing) emphasizes the need for merchandising and business results. In reality, probably both viewpoints should be serviced. The best way to attend to these divergent business outcomes is to learn people's expectations right before the event, so that during a post-promotion analysis, everyone is using the same evaluation criteria.

2. Expectations Must Evolve into Specific Plans and Measurable Results

While most people acknowledge that this is a standard business practice, somehow this standard practice frequently disappears when it comes to special events. A plan must be developed as a result of clear expectations that will be specific, measurable, achievable, and compatible (SMAC) within the organization's capacity.

Rich George, President of Exsportise, really lives by this belief. This small but emerging sports marketing company is experiencing phenomenal business success. Mr. George explains:

> Sports and special events marketing companies must be most concerned with measuring results for clients. Additionally, clients should be more concerned about becoming involved with programs that will produce results! It has been a comfortable environment for quite some time for sports and special events companies to shy away from the development of measurements and the promising of results. Companies always fall back on the notion that advertising and special events are too abstract to measure and thus difficult to quantify. They instead fall back on emotion and gut feeling. I don't disagree with the need for the use of business instinct, but it should be complemented with analysis of whether or not the event helped with actual business results.
>
> Business results need to be measured in two categories. The first category is the hard business results category, which is comprised of an analysis of sales, share, profit, and the variables that contributed to the failure or success of these. The other measurement is in the area of soft results. Soft results are categorized by measuring how successful the hospitality function was, or how well the program was implemented and executed. In essence, hard results are objectively measured, and soft results are subjectively measured. At Exsportise, we go to great lengths to not only measure hard business results but also soft business results.
>
> An example that comes to mind happened a couple of years ago. I was responsible for the development and implementation of a series of professional-amateur-celebrity tennis tournaments. I did this on behalf of a particular product and had very little trouble

analyzing the hard business results within each of the markets. I also went to work in trying to analyze the soft business results and focused on primarily the hospitality function. To further quantify this perceivably subjective side of the program, I sent a survey to all of our customers who were involved with the hospitality program around these events. The response was strong, with over 50 percent of the participants reacting. I quickly discovered that the tennis teaching clinics that the company perceived as being the primary highlights of the program was in effect an abysmal failure. Very few people participated in the clinics at all, and very few could offer any ways to improve this aspect of the program. On the other hand, we had a pro-celebrity talent show one evening during the program, and this feature received a 4.6 scale rating with the highest possible grade being a 5.0. I also invited survey respondents to include verbatims to give the results some texture and was stunned by the comments surrounding the pro-celebrity talent show. I continually saw comments indicating that this was some of the best entertainment they'd ever seen in their lives and strongly thanked and appreciated the sponsoring brand for providing this element of hospitality.

In summary, it is very important to set objectives and then measure your company's performance against these objectives. One way to look at the absence of measurements is that you can never fail. However, eventually the absence of understanding could ruin some very good programs.

3. Special Events Programs Should Be Designed with the User in Mind

Keep the programs simple for the sales organization, the customer, and the consumer. Fight the temptation to make this program the "program of the century." Remember what was stated earlier in the chapter; "To do everything is to do nothing," and that certainly holds true with special events.

4. Keep the Events Product Expandable

If you develop a special event that will work well for a couple of brands, then can it work well for four or five brands? Eventually, you reach a point of diminishing return when you involve so many brands that their identification with the event becomes blurred. However, this needs to be evaluated on an event-by-event basis. Generally, it is also subject to the individual brand strategies. If a brand is well established and is trying to compete regionally without having to discount price, then five or six of these type brands together would benefit from a special event promotion. On the other hand, if you have a brand that is in dire need of consumer awareness, then this brand should sponsor the program alone or possibly with one other complementary product. Brands that need awareness ought to be the most sensitive about clutter.

It is very important to make the distinction at this point that I am talking about one company with a "stable" of brands. I am also talking about special events that have company as well as category exclusivity. An example of this type of program is the previously mentioned Barnum & Bailey Circus promotion. Procter & Gamble, with several brands, underwrote this program exclusively. This program became brand expandable because Barnum & Bailey and Procter & Gamble had an exclusive relationship.

Many special events are programs that attract several different corporate sponsors: for example, the Moscow Marathon. Several different companies become involved with the sponsorship and marketing of their programs behind this event. It is up to the participating companies to leverage this relationship with the Moscow Marathon to give their program the advantage. Because of category exclusivity clauses, you usually don't have promotion clutter. Critics would be hard pressed to say that the marketing effort of the official sneaker of the Moscow Marathon had a negative impact (promotion clutter) on the official hotel. In fact, oftentimes synergies can develop that can work to the advantage of different products and companies all under the umbrella of one focal special event.

In essence, when you review special event opportunities, analyze whether or not you have the flexibility of expanding the number of brands (that you control) within a program. This, as you can imagine, can become very efficient, and helps spread out the cost of involvement.

5. Look for Events that Are Long-Term

The most expense and energy that will ever be committed to special events usually happens during year one. Because of the heavy initial work be cautious of involvement with special events that are one-shot deals or look like short-term propositions. Of course, there are some notable exceptions like the Olympics, which happen once every four years and are always in a different city. If the price was right, I would still try to develop a program around the Olympics, but I would be very choosy about what products became involved. You really want to develop long-term relationships that can be repeatable if you are successful. If this occurs you will be "grandfathered" in the event and it will be tough for competition to dislodge you.

6. The Event Should Enhance Your Brand's and Customer's Image

You want to do the right things for your brands and customer relationships. Be cautious to protect the integrity of these customer relationships and brand images by being associated with events that would only reflect positively on your involvement.

7. If at All Possible, Think Big

If you have the organizational capacity, bigger in special events is generally better. Again, it really does depend on the situation your brand is in and the market of the special event. But basically, I would rather have a very successful special event that really related to a large marketing area rather than a strong event that related to a sub-market. I understand that sometimes the sum of the individual parts far exceeds the value of the whole. With that in mind, manage this carefully, because your organization may not have the capacity to efficiently manage several little programs, and it would be better for you to become involved in a broader-based program. An example of this usually occurs in the area of radio promoting. Radio stations are very good at developing local events for companies, and I frequently took advantage of them. However, I usually became involved with radio stations only in major markets that had a strong signal and could cover some of the adjacent sub-markets. That way, I dealt with fewer but larger radio stations, and my promotion generally had broader consumer and customer reach. Remember, however, that this situation depends upon a company's resources. Smaller regional companies may be better advised to utilize smaller radio stations and newspapers because the economics fall closer within that company's comfort zone.

8. The Event Should Eventually Pay Out

As previously discussed, it is tough to ascertain whether or not payout has been achieved. Payout occurs when the financial investment in the event is offset by enough incremental product sales to cover the investment. Basically, though, it is important to develop a financial plan wherein you know, based upon sales and profit, whether or not this event contributed toward furthering your business objectives.

I write very guardedly on this topic, because I have found severe contradiction on this point. Almost every marketer I spoke with insisted upon short-term/immediate payout for any event involving their product group. Most salespeople I spoke with hoped for short-term payout, but believed an event should be given more than one year to financially prove itself. The contradiction arises because generally the marketing people are more long-term-oriented than the salespeople. Yet when it comes to special events and their payout, the tables are reversed. The issue here is ownership because marketers feel that special events are gifts given to the sales force and cease to own them shortly after program development. A better plan is for both sales and marketing to own the event.

THE EVENT IS A PRODUCT!

It is important for marketers to understand what sales already knows regarding special events. Sellers view a special event program as a product. Marketers view the special event as almost anything but a product. The notion that a special event is a product is an important one. If people agree that the event/ program is truly a product, then most reasonable people will give a product more than one opportunity to survive. Certainly, if a new automobile or brand of chocolate syrup were introduced, those tangible goods would be given more than one chance to succeed. So, too, should special events; and to that end, people should not demand that events pay for themselves during year one. It is my earnest hope that most events will pay for themselves quickly because, unlike introducing new automobiles and chocolate syrups, a special event usually is not a capital-intensive proposition.

I recently spoke with a senior executive at a major sports marketing firm, who privately confided that clients' demand for instant success hinder the marketing agency from recommending program elements that would best serve the long-term future of the event. He did suggest that the problem is somewhat of an organizational issue in that client companies rotate their people (some planned, some through attrition) so frequently that it is tough to develop continuity and long-term relationships built through experience and trust. Instead, the reality of short-term relationships has as its byproduct lack of continuity, and this creates a demand for quick success.

The issue of payout is similar to the issue of measurement. As you would expect, payout is one aspect of measuring the success or failure of a special event, and there are both hard and soft payouts. Rich George, in his previous comments, took significant steps to try to quantify the issue of soft measurements. This too can be done with the soft payouts of special events. When it comes to hard payout, three simple calculations can aid you with your analysis. The first and second calculations, which focus on sales and share, are very fundamental. The third calculation, which focuses on determining profit and loss, is more involved (but not intellectually complicated). Case 3A and the accompanying narrative will explain the thinking and calculations to determine sales and share impact as well as profit and loss.

While this scenario closely resembles one that did occur, the actual details (share, sales, profit) have been altered to show the calculations and analysis process, and to protect the confidentiality of the product and company.

CASE 3A

Sales/Share Calculation (and shallow analysis)
Background

An automobile company was involved with a sports-related special event during the month of September, 1990. The entire dealer network in a large market tied in strongly with the event by running a regional promotion (sweepstakes related) and regional advertising (print and radio). The dealer network chose to target a particular type of automobile for their promotion. Remember, principle number four suggests that if this program proves successful, they may want to add one or two more target models of automobiles to this promotion next year.

The following data was needed to appropriately evaluate the sales, share, and trend impact of the regional program:

1. Dealer network target model car sales by month for 1989 and 1990.

	Jan.	Feb.	Mar.	Apr.	May	June	July	Aug.	Sep.	Oct.	Nov.	Dec.
1990	19	31	40	49	50	39	45	45	79	60	35	52
1989	25	31	31	47	42	51	47	52	52	31	27	49

2. Total sales by month within the particular target category by all dealers (include competition) in the region for 1989 and 1990.

	Jan.	Feb.	Mar.	Apr.	May	June	July	Aug.	Sep.	Oct.	Nov.	Dec.
1990	60	64	76	100	101	94	90	97	134	115	91	100
1989	62	70	65	80	94	100	107	106	109	79	75	83

Calculation Narrative

To determine the impact this event had on sales, you need to perform simple index calculations. These calculations should be done to analyze both how the company performed compared with itself and with the overall category. To calculate the index for how this event performed, divide 1990 sales for the months of September through December by 1989 sales for the same months of September through December. If you want to measure the sales trends leading up to the event, divide the individual months of January through August 1990 by January through August 1989. Don't just go by the aggregate calculation because aggregate analysis for a period often obscures an obvious trend. Pay attention to any monthly trends. An aggregate comparison for January through August 1990 with January through August 1989 could look great but hide the fact of a declining sales trend since May.

> *Author's Note: When reviewing analysis, remember that the author's choice of "analysis method" can often sculpt the results. Regrettably, agendas have been reshaped by analysis that was technically correct, yet one dimensional at best. First, I always try to understand the possible motives of the person doing the analysis. If the person doing the review has been the owner and leader of the program, then it is natural to want to make the effort look as favorable as possible. It's always tough to review your own program and pronounce its failure. Remember, figures never lie, but liars sometimes figure!*

Sales Index Analysis					
	Sept.	Oct.	Nov.	Dec.	Sept.–Dec. Aggregate
1990	79	60	35	52	226
1989	52	31	27	49	159
Variance	(+27)	(+29)	(+8)	(+3)	(+67)
Sales Index	152	194	130	106	142

As you can see, the promotion had an impressive immediate impact on sales during the promotion month and positively affected sales in the following two months.

	Jan.	Feb.	Mar.	Apr.	May	June	July	Aug.	Jan.–Aug. Aggregate
					Sales Trend Analysis				
1990	19	31	40	49	50	39	45	45	318
1989	25	31	31	47	42	51	47	52	326
Variance	(−6)	(−)	(+9)	(+2)	(+8)	(−12)	(−2)	(−7)	(−8)
Sales Index	76	100	129	104	119	76	96	87	98

From a trend basis, this data shows that the four-month aggregate sales index during the promotion evaluation period was 142. This is in contrast to the eight months prior to the regional event when aggregate sales indexed at 98.

To determine share, simply divide the luxury automobile company's actual sales by the total sales of the luxury category. For share calculation purposes, we will just look at 1990.

Share Analysis

	Sept.	Oct.	Nov.	Dec.	Aggregate Sept.–Dec.
Luxury Automobile dealer network sales	79	60	35	52	226
Total Luxury Automobile category including dealer network and competition	134	115	91	100	440
Actual share (of all sales)	60%	52%	38%	52%	51%

The Luxury Automobile Company network experienced strong share improvement in September and October. Share slipped in November, but this may have been a result of competition launching a defensive program. The company regained share again in December. Total sum share for the four-month promotion was a strong 51 percent.

In the absolute, market share of all Luxury automobiles rose from 47 percent (January through August 1990) to 51 percent (September through December 1990). This resulted in a share index of 109.

There is much more analysis that can be done with this sales and share information. It would also be appropriate to

									Aggregate
	Jan.	Feb.	Mar.	Apr.	May	June	July	Aug.	Jan.–Aug.
Luxury Automobile dealer network sales	19	31	40	49	50	39	45	45	318
Total Luxury Automobile category including dealer network and competition	60	64	76	100	101	94	90	97	682
Actual Share (of all sales)	32%	48%	53%	49%	50%	41%	50%	46%	47%

Share Trend Analysis

integrate into the analysis a calculation to understand the sales and share results for the company's other markets. These markets (we'll say this is a domestic U.S. analysis) would be called "balance United States" and would serve as a large control market to further evaluate this promotion. Using a control market to compare with your regional effort is a good way to see if the regional promotion outperformed the national promotion.

While the sales and share numbers look positive behind this regional special event, the real test will be the test calculation to understand if it was profitable.

Profit and Loss Calculation

Using this automobile example, we need to look at the actual sales difference between September through December 1989 and September through December 1990. Our previous review indicates that the dealer network sold 67 more cars during this period in 1990 than in 1989. This increase in sales can probably be attributed to the regional event barring any strong aberrations in either the 1989 September through December base or the 1990 September through December period. (Special note: Sometimes you have to go back one year to correct for sales aberrations.)

This automobile sold for an average of $37,000 during September through December 1990. Once *all* the costs (manufacturing, marketing, sales, and other overheads) were assigned, the total cost was $31,000. This left a gross profit of $6,000 per car.

	$37,000	average retail cost per car
(Less)	− 31,000	average cost per car
	$6,000	profit per car

The total cost of the regional special event was $150,000.

	$402,000	gross profit (67 incremental cars times $6,000 profit per car)
(Less)	− 150,000	total cost of special event
	$252,000	net profit
	$3,761	net profit per car ($252,000 ÷ 67)

	$150,000	total cost of special event
÷	67	incremental cars sold
	$2,239	cost per incremental sale

It is up to management to evaluate the economics of this promotion. The evaluation parameters should reveal the cost and profit per incremental sale. Simply said, did the investment behind this promotion meet or exceed the needed volume and profit from this effort?

On the surface, this promotion would seem to be strong from an incremental sales and share review as well as profit contribution.

Whenever the promotion meets or exceeds its financial objectives (it is also assumed that the objectives will at least break even), payout generally has been achieved.

Before the book is closed for 1990 on this promotion, a soft factor review should be conducted to give the analysis some balance. Of primary interest would be a customer survey to learn whether the awareness generated by the special event was the key factor in customers' visiting the dealership.

The need to eventually produce payout for a program is fundamentally correct. You can't maintain involvement with programs that make you feel good yet don't support your business. The only exception to this are charity and contributory programs. Sometimes a company is very wise not to myopically focus on the bottom-line impact of an event if it is civically and morally the right long-term special event to become involved in. However, these programs are few and must be balanced heavily with fiscal responsibility and strategic alignment.

9. You Can Always Improve a Program

The principle of improving a program appears in several other discussions within this book. Don't rest on your past successes, whether is is a regional or national effort that you're involved in. Always try to find ways to improve your event. As mentioned in a previous example, if there are 10 elements to a special event program and this year you can only do 3 of them in a first-class manner, then be prepared next year to do 4 or 5 in a first-class manner. With special events, experience is the great equalizer. Through experience comes expanded capacity, and through expanded capacity comes the opportunity to improve.

10. Decide Whether the Event Should Be Managed In-House or Out-of-House

As a rule, I recommend that special events be (at least) executionally managed by an out-of-house agency. This generalization is made with the assumption that most companies do not have special events as a primary/dominant marketing focus. If special events is a principal direction, then you might want to consider having a special events functional specialist in-house. An important reason to pay for outside expertise (usually 15 to 25 percent of overall program budget) is continuity. If you retain a reputable special events company, you can assume they will not fail based upon personal turnover. Special events is this company's main mission; it is probably not your company's main mission. When companies bring special events in-house, they usually underestimate the size of staff needed to execute a quality program. They frequently understaff, frustrate the function, and eventually create turnover, which, with a small staff, can be terminal.

For those companies that want to progress toward in-house management, the following case study demonstrates the appropriate conditions.

BRINGING PRODUCTION IN-HOUSE: A CORPORATE CASE STUDY

(Courtesy of Special Events Report, 213 West Institute Place, Suite 303, Chicago, Illinois 60610)

"Sponsors of five or more events should consider becoming producers and owners. Special event managers should not just be purchasing agents." That's advice from O'Neill, Inc., the California wetsuit and sportswear manufacturer with worldwide sales of $100 million, which took production and promotion of the company's events in-house.

In 1987, senior management evaluated the company's 13-year involvement with sponsorship, which has included more than 50 events, mostly in water sports. The question was not whether to continue—it was a given that sponsorship allowed the company to communicate its product attributes and image to a targeted audience—but rather what form the company's association should take in the future.

The company had produced the MARUI/O'NEILL MAUI INVITATIONAL stop on the Pro Boardsailing Assn. tour since 1980. And it was seriously considering forming an in-house agency to produce and promote other events it sponsored.

Control of the O'Neill image was the central issue, according to David Miller, the company's sports marketing director.

> Image is our greatest asset and it's the artistic style points around an event that drive the image home to consumers.
>
> Outside producers can put up bleachers and get competitors on the water, but the real bang for the buck comes with innovative merchandising and style points. Inevitably, the guy who is best at handling event logistics is not best at handling the image side of things.

Concern with image led to a time-consuming involvement with producers and agencies that in turn put a strain on upper management, Miller said.

Events demand play-by-play judgment calls on the part of the sponsor, especially if the company is serious about having a promotional impact. The producers knew we were terribly image-conscious, and they didn't feel confident making certain decisions on our behalf, so they required a lot of steering. It finally became a case of too many vice presidents getting too many calls for too many low-priority issues.

Should the company give the producers more freedom or take events in-house? Negative experiences with producers in the past and the nature of the sports in which O'Neill was involved made the decision clear-cut. "The lack of maturity of the water sports industry means there is no full-service entity you can turn to and say 'We want penetration into surfing, boardsailing, or waterskiing'; without that entity, water sports are postured for takeover."

Realizing that other sponsors were in the same position when it came to the lack of one-stop shopping for water sports involvements, O'Neill management saw the opportunity to use an in-house agency to serve other sponsors.

Other factors in O'Neill's favor included a stable of more than 100 athletes, advertising leverage with water sports publications, strong relationships with sanctioning bodies, a broad base of subcontractor contacts from previous sponsorships and in-house video, graphics, and advertising departments.

In November 1987, the company formed O'Neill Sports Marketing to design, develop, implement, promote, and oversee O'Neill events. It is a separate profit center within O'Neill, Inc.'s structure.

Marketing vs. Logistics

The five-person department began with two full-time staffers. Fifteen employees from the 100-person headquarters staff provide support.

O'Neill concentrates on the marketing and promotion aspects of events, using 150 subcontractors to enhance its in-house capabilities in areas that require additional geographic, governmental, and logistical expertise. "From a practical standpoint, there's no way we can pull off the biggest event on Maui without mobilizing a local effort," Miller said. "While logistics are critical to our success, it is a connect-the-dots business. Marketing and promotion is the real crux; the creativity involved is what we want to control ourselves."

The decision to be marketing-oriented kept O'Neill's upfront investment small. New expenses of the department, which operates on a $2.5 million budget, were confined to hiring employees and buying office equipment.

"If we were going to position ourselves as a full-service agency, we had to hire seasoned marketers. We had to avoid the trap of starting too small and looking like a banner-hanger. Hiring hardworking, organized, enthusiastic people wasn't enough," Miller said.

Although the department's focus is on marketing rather than logistics, certain functions had to be accommodated. For example, storage space was an unanticipated issue. In addition to O'Neill banners and merchandise, the department's office became a shipping and receiving point for other sponsors' promotional materials.

Another early surprise was an overloaded phone system. As contact point for all aspects of their events, O'Neill needed to enlist answering services and upgrade its voice-mail system to accommodate calls from athletes, ticket requests, and merchandise orders.

Working with Cosponsors

Among O'Neill's objectives in forming the department was "enhancing the promotional impact of our events through development of value-added cosponsor relationships."

While cosponsors provide business for its in-house graphics division and help offset O'Neill's cost to stage the events, the company's primary interest in recruiting cosponsors is cross-promotion possibilities.

For example, O'Neill, which acts as producer, promoter, title sponsor, and sponsorship agency of surfing's Cold Water

Classic, brought in Pepsi-Cola to co-title the February event. The soft drink's involvement allowed the event to be promoted in over 300 7-Eleven Food Stores in the Bay area through point of sales displays, merchandise offers, a sweepstakes, and posters. Pepsi-Cola also tagged local radio spots, an area in which O'Neill spends no money.

O'Neill's ownership position can be a strong selling point with cosponsors, Miller said. For example, Adolph Coors Co. dropped its sponsorship of the Cold Water Classic in November, less than four months before the event was to occur. "Pepsi normally makes decisions on a long timeline," Miller said. "The people we met with told us their willingness to turn the opportunity around in three months rather than 18 was because the event was an in-house project and we had a vested interest in its success."

O'Neill promises each cosponsor that it will quantify the promotional impact of every event on that company's terms. This commitment is considerably more time-intensive than anyone realizes. "Keeping up that sponsor dialogue consumes a lot of our resources," Miller said. "We spend a lot of time measuring exposure in newspapers and evaluating ID on broadcasts."

Sports Marketing also opens its books to cosponsors. Turning a profit is not a primary objective of the department, Miller said. "We don't run in the black. Our job is to reduce expenditures each year and get more bang for the buck."

O'Neill's long-term plan is to extend its sponsor partnerships beyond water sports. Pepsi-Cola has already hired O'Neill to design apparel and logos for its Collegiate Volleyball Classic. The two companies are also discussing production of a tour in another sport. Growth will also come through expansion of existing events, such as adding a music component to the O'NEILL/PEPSI COLD WATER CLASSIC.

Riding Waves with Licensees and Retailers

Sports Marketing is also bringing image consistency to events sponsored by its licensees and retailers. For example, the

O'NEILL/IMB SURFING MASTERS in Australia is produced and promoted by Skima, O'Neill's Australian licensee. Miller's department advises Skima on sponsorship negotiations, collateral design, production, and event promotion.

At times, O'Neill's role varies within the same circuit. For example, Marui Co., one of Japan's largest retailers, is a four-year, mid-seven-figure cosponsor of a three-stop windsurfing series held in Hawaii, Japan, and California. O'Neill is producer and promoter of the Hawaii stop of the MARUI/O'NEILL WORLD TOUR OF WINDSURFING and acts as consultant to Marui on collateral and other event-related materials. At the Japanese stop, Marui acts as producer and promoter, and O'Neill consults on the event's competitive content and on-site merchandising and sponsor visibility.

For the San Francisco event, O'Neill is producer and promoter and acts as liaison for Marui's broadcast crew, which films the event for Japanese TV. The film is also known in the activewear department at Marui stores, where O'Neill apparel is prominently featured.

In the few cases where O'Neill has kept sponsorship of other producers' events (e.g., the COORS LIGHT WATERSKI TOUR) the manufacturer relies on its own people to maximize on-site signage, merchandising, and promotion opportunities. For example, O'Neill, secondary sponsor of the pro ski tour for the last three years, schedules interviews and photo sessions with Team O'Neill waterskiers at each stop.

O'Neill keeps separate accounts for each event and prorates overhead among them. This provides an accurate picture of how much each event spends and earns. "We push as much of the costs out to the events as possible," Miller said. "That way we can review their economic performance. Internal overhead is kept to about $400,000."

O'Neill, which sponsors a single event or minitour in a sport rather than spreading its resources over many events, is planning a snowboard minitour with World Cup events in Japan, Europe, and the United States for 1990. Future plans also include production of the Super Skins of Waterskiing, a made-for-broadcast invitational scheduled for September 1991.[1]

Case Study Epilogue

An Interesting Twist

I recently contacted David Miller, who is heavily referenced in the case study. My intention was to learn how O'Neill had progressed over the last three or more years with their in-house special events program. What I found out was very interesting and supportive of my original contention in point 10. That is, when special events cease to become a main mission, they should probably be assigned to an out-of-house expert.

David Miller is now a principal of the full-service sports marketing company called Sport Link, located in Capitola, California. Mr. Miller indicated that

> The in-house special events management program that O'Neill conducted worked brilliantly for the past three years. However, a "game change" took place during the late summer of 1990 that created a strategic mismatch for O'Neill and their in-house management and expansion of special events.
>
> O'Neill made a decision to buy back their sportswear licensing agreement for their United States domestic business. When they took this license back from another company, they suspended the license as O'Neill was not quite ready to gear up to become an apparel manufacturer. O'Neill's international business has done very well, and all of the international licenses have been maintained. However, with the suspension of the O'Neill sportswear license in the United States, it meant that O'Neill domestically was only primarily selling and marketing wet suits. Special events programming was targeted to advance the apparel business as well as other corporate relationships. Special events marketing did extremely well to develop brand awareness and early

---

[1] "Bringing Production In-House: A Corporate Case Study," *Special Events Report*, May 29, 1989, pp. 4–5.

continuity of purchase. As O'Neill has restructured to manage their license suspension, they no longer needed to utilize special events in a growth mode focus. O'Neill certainly has not retreated from special events. In fact, they still have three large programs that they conduct annually. However, because of this licensing adjustment relationship, their special events program could not provide the value added function that it needed.

Mr. Miller further added that he recommended that the special events function now be shifted out-of-house since the company was only primarily engaged in three special events. The company agreed and is working a blend of some in-house management and some out-of-house management.

Mr. Miller indicates that the principles and beliefs used to establish the O'Neill in-house special events marketing program were fundamentally strong and that because they had an evaluation process built into their business plan, they could quickly react to this major licensing issue. Mr. Miller recommends that any company with five or more special events and a total budget of $1.5 million should start looking internally for special event management. This is not automatic but is a guideline that should trigger some consideration. With this guideline in place, it was the right decision for O'Neill to depart from their three-year program and make the decision they made.

SUMMARY

Special events can be a complementary tactic to regional marketing. In fact, many people would argue that special events and/or local promotions is the essence of regional marketing. I strongly disagree with that notion because regional marketing is much more. I do not suggest an unflattering subordination of special events. Instead, I believe that until you become competent with special events, you can never become a full-service regional marketer.

SUMMARY CHECKLIST

1. *Are the general expectations of the event clear between sales and marketing before the event?*

2. *Have your expectations been translated into specific plans and measurable business results?*

3. *Have you kept your special events program user friendly?*

4. *If this event is successful for one or two brands, can more brands be added to it and maintain an equivalent level of success?*

5. *Does the event have long-term potential?*

6. *Does the event enhance our brand and customer's image?*

7. *When it comes to special events, are you thinking big whenever possible?*

8. *Will the event pay out now or in the near future and in hard business terms?*

9. *Are you continually seeking out ways to improve your program?*

10. *Should the special event be managed in-house or out-of-house?*

Regional Marketing Principles

A s powerful a strategy as regional marketing truly is, there are many ways to go astray. A simple way to harness the benefits and manage the risk is by understanding some important principles.

This section covers general principles as they relate to regional marketing at large. These principles are appropriate for both product and service industries. Within the framework of general principles, the following topics will be discussed:

1. Empowerment of the regional marketer.
2. Who should be a regional marketer.
3. How that person should be trained.
4. The right conditions and support systems.

This section will also go beyond *general* principles and focus on specific principles as they relate to some elements of the marketing mix:

1. Promotion.
2. Pricing.
3. Advertising (given special treatment "outside" of promotion).
4. Product and distribution.

Hopefully, a thorough understanding of these principles will produce a regional marketing blueprint. Development and execution of a regional marketing plan is something that should be carefully crafted. If quality time is spent on the "front end" (principles), then the results will be worthwhile.

Chapter Four

General Principles

INTRODUCTION

Most sellers, marketers, and educators whom I interviewed agreed that principles of regional marketing needed to be clearly discussed in this book. During the course of my interviews, I noticed a real absence of this awareness. Most of the people, if pushed, would brainstorm on principles within the marketing mix elements of price, advertising, promotion, and product. While it is important to have principles for the marketing mix items, it is vital to have an understanding of general principles on the subject of regional marketing.

GENERAL PRINCIPLES ARE FUNDAMENTAL TRUTHS

These truths are learned from experience. I sincerely wish that when I started my regional marketing experience, there had been an existing framework of principles to help do my job. Instead, I, and the majority of the people interviewed for the book, had never grasped the general principles about how to do regional marketing successfully.

Again principles are fundamental truths, and there are several important regional marketing principles:

1. Empowerment principles.
2. Recruitment principles.

3. Training principles.

4. Information principles.

5. Timing/location principles.

EMPOWERMENT PRINCIPLES

During an interview recently, I was asked what the most important principle of regional marketing was. I responded that if I could be granted one wish only, that wish would be that regional marketers be empowered. My preference is to have an empowered, moderately trained person operating regional marketing rather than a well-trained, powerless regional marketer.

Empowerment is a necessary first step for all that follows. An empowered regional marketing manager is one who has been independently financed with an operating budget and democratically ratified and blessed by upper management. These two elements of empowerment are very dependent upon one another and should be considered a package deal. I speak from personal experience that to be half-empowered creates chaos, poor job satisfaction, and wastes incredible time and resources.

As one of the early regional marketing managers for Procter & Gamble, I was half-empowered. I was blessed by upper management, yet remained unfunded for my programs. This created a situation of immense frustration. In fact, every request for money that I made seemed to take on overwhelming complexity and concern. Over time (through internal selling), I succeeded in attracting several million dollars towards my pricing, promotion, and advertising programs. However, it took so much time to sell the centralized marketing and sales systems that on several occasions the funding was provided months after the ideal window of opportunity passed. Because the window had somewhat closed, the programs themselves became more difficult to adjust and then subsequently execute in the field.

There is a saying in real estate that the three most important elements of selling a house are "location, location, and location." The parallel to regional marketing is that the three most important principles of regional marketing (and regional management) are empowerment, empowerment, and empowerment! For management to empower, a certain level of trust and confidence must exist. This can happen if management believes that regional marketers have been well picked and trained. With that statement as background, let me now make a transition to the next regional marketing principle.

RECRUITMENT PRINCIPLES

The Dechert-Hampe & Company surveyed manufacturing companies that represented over $111 billion in sales. One of the questions asked in the survey was "What type of person would be most effective in a regional marketing position?" The response is not surprising and is shown by Figure 4–1.

This 8 out of 10 attraction to a new hybrid manager is a significant change from the past. Most companies historically have segregated their sales and marketing departments rather than integrating them. Because of the ever-changing and highly competitive business environment, the need for a hybrid manager exists. To properly execute regional marketing, you need the benefit of this hybrid type. The manager of the future needs to be less of a specialist and more of a generalist. However, that does not mean that the regional marketing manager, sales manager, and product manager should become mediocre in more areas of concentration instead of strong in one or two areas.

In Chapter Two, I extensively discussed sales and marketing differences and their fragile strategic relationship. Both disciplines should feed the regional marketing position.

FIGURE 4–1
The Hybrid Manager

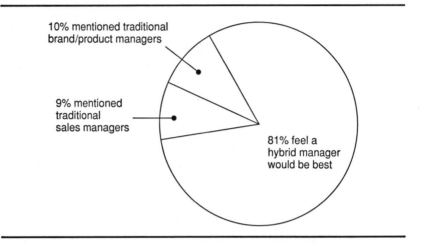

10% mentioned traditional brand/product managers

9% mentioned traditional sales managers

81% feel a hybrid manager would be best

Source: Michael Raffini, "Regional Marketing: Survey Shows Accelerating Interest," *DHC Viewpoint* (Dechert-Hampe & Company, Winter 1987–88), pp. 1–2.

Target Training Zone

Following is an organizational chart of a typical sales and marketing company. The regional marketing manager subject to the commitment level of the company should be inserted into the management hierarchy in one of two ways. The first way is Figure 4–2. If the company cannot make a decision to staff the regional marketing function, then unit sales managers and/or region sales managers ought to be significantly trained in the discipline. On the brand side, assistant brand managers and brand managers should be coached and trained.

Appropriate Level

In Figure 4–3, it is assumed that the company has made a conscious choice to staff the regional marketing position. In this case, subject to the commitment of the company, the regional marketing should be introduced somewhere in the zone

Figure 4–2
Sales and Marketing Career Paths

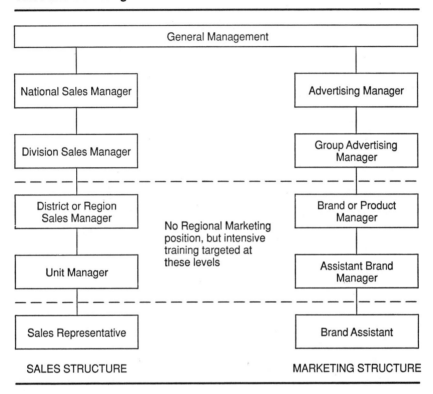

between sales unit manager/assistant brand manager and sales division manager/group advertising manager. My personal point of view is that most mid- to large-size companies ought to have their regional marketing manager at the same level as the region sales manager and product/brand manager. Possibly, I would adjust this in an upward fashion if the budget responsibility also encompassed an integration of profit.

There is a difference between job expansion and job enrichment. Within that mind-set, there should be a situation of solid job enrichment for a region sales manager and/or a brand/product manager to move into the position of regional marketing manager in a lateral fashion (or slight upgrade) after their current assignments. This transition seems logical, because it

Figure 4–3
Sales and Marketing Career Paths

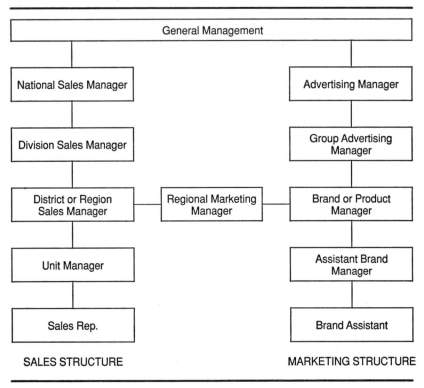

would be the first formal integration of the sales and marketing discipline within the respective organization, other than through previous cross-training experiences.

Because I don't want this book to be a compromise, I will deal with the scenario of one regional marketing position available with two equally qualified candidates for the position, one from brand management and one from sales. I will qualify my comments by indicating that there should not be much downside risk in highly qualified people coming from either discipline. However, if your company is a traditional sales and marketing company that is strongly consumer-focused (consumer-focused means targeted to the ultimate buyer of your good or service), then the marketing person should be chosen. If your company is becoming more customer (trade/retail outlet) focused, then the salesperson should receive the position. The way you manage your staffing risk is by having a competent training and onboarding program.

Reporting Lines

This is a tough decision that is dependent on regional marketing conditions. The four primary conditions relative to reporting lines are:

1. Charter. What kind of charter has been established for these regional marketing managers? Are they primarily advertisers? Are they primarily concerned with price and promotion? Are they intended to be fully operational and empowered in all areas?

2. Location. Where will the regional marketing manager operate from? Will this person be field based or central office based?

3. Budget consideration. Will the regional marketing manager have a well-funded, autonomous budget or one subject to the individual brand or department budgets?

4. Career pathing. In most companies, this position would either be under the authority of the brand/marketing organization or sales department. Some companies do not have much flexibility relative to "crossing between" the different departments. Will your company "bust" its paradigms and allow for a "corporate gender neutral" level?

All four of these conditions must be addressed to determine the extremely important question of reporting lines for the regional marketing manager. Since I do advocate that the regional marketing position be filled by either a region sales manager (some companies call this district manager) and/or a marketing brand manager, management responsibility for the regional marketing manager should be at the group advertising and/or division sales manager level. Personally, I am not a fan of matrix management, wherein exists both straight-line and dotted-line authority. However, in the case of the regional marketing manager, subject to company structure and conditions, matrix management might work.

The issue of reporting lines is a critical decision to make very early in the process of developing regional marketing. This is essential, based upon the tenet of ownership. As with the development of a simple regional marketing promotion, the development of a regional marketing corporate program needs an owner. Of course, it would be very wise to develop regional marketing from a combined sales and marketing approach, but one department must be chosen to ride point.

TRAINING PRINCIPLES

The challenge here is to recognize the different strengths and weaknesses of the sales and marketing departments. The appropriate training approach is to bring sales and marketing together. Focus on common strengths and liabilities to develop an on-target training program. This program shouldn't create a condition of half of the group (sales) not listening while the marketers learn about sales issues, and vice versa.

Cross-Training

The way to adjust for this is by cross-training. This integrated training program, wherein sellers train marketers and marketers train sellers, is not new but has gained momentum in the past few years. John T. Thomas, a partner in the Chicago office of Ward Howell International, Inc., talked about "the growing importance of cross-training" in a recent *New York Times* article.[1] His general conclusion was that the majority of top executives in years to come will have been cross-trained. I emphatically agree!

The second way to maintain training focus is by keeping your training class size small. From my experience, having

---

[1] Elizabeth M. Fowler, "Salespeople Also Trained in Marketing," *The New York Times* (August 15, 1989), p. D-18.

6 to 10 participants is ideal; two weeks is on-target for initial orientation. In a broader sense, it seems that it takes about one to two years of on-the-job experience before regional marketing establishes its own culture and identity. This doesn't mean that you have to wait one to two years for programs to work. However, it is important for the success of any new program to have expectations that are manageable. A full six-month cross-training experience should also take place, commencing soon after the two-week orientation. Salespeople ought to work in the product groups, and product people ought to work in the sales discipline. Once this training program takes place, an individually customized program of transition from the central office to the field location should take place.

Training Road Map

I have tried to set up the flow of this book to be generally consistent with the flow of a training program. Specifically, Section I deals with regional marketing's current state. This section defines the topic and demands a general understanding of the evolution of regional marketing. A training discussion of the different styles of regional marketing needs to take place to add substance and flexibility to the topic. Since regional marketing is not all positive, trainees need a quick up-front discussion of clash of cultures and centralized versus decentralized marketing. Lastly in the introductory section, a review needs to occur regarding different ongoing company regional marketing experiences. Newly appointed regional marketing managers need to know that (even without their discipline being formalized) local programs are probably still underway.

It is important at this stage to set up the transition towards a focus in Section II on regional marketing principles. This transition occurs more comfortably when company regional marketing experiences are discussed that are from several business categories and industries. For example, it is important to recognize that regional marketing also takes place in the airline industry, fastfood business, automobile business, as well as many other disciplines.

Trainees should come away from their first module (section I) with a general orientation which should build toward an overall excitement about the topic.

General Principles

Section II of the book focuses on principles that are the fundamental truths. So too should the next phase of training. The discussion of principles needs to go from macro focus to micro focus. General principles need to be understood by the trainees and then marketing mix principles need to be mastered. Much time should be spent on the particular marketing mix principles. It is important for new regional marketers to have a thorough understanding of the principles so that they can start to understand strategies and tactics.

Regional Marketing Assessment Process

Section III works well as a complement to the previous section (training module, if you will) of principles. Both Section II and Section III provide a well-rounded basis of understanding for an actual and/or hypothetical case study exercise that should occur in Section IV. As mentioned in the introduction of this book, at this point, we begin to apply what we have learned and shift from a process point of view to a product/results orientation. Developing regional brand strategies and customer-ized marketing takes much time and discussion and will still not become second nature for most managers by the end of this training program. Instead, participants must pursue this key transition state (from process to product) so that they can understand that regional marketing is more than an intellectual exercise; in effect, it is a results-oriented program.

At this stage of the development process, I hope that people have a broad understanding of regional marketing and an honest commitment and understanding that regional marketing can work to better most business situations. Additionally, people should leave with a template that they can refer to as they engage in the cross-training process for the next six months.

INFORMATION PRINCIPLE

The Information Principle has three primary components:

1. Analytical/survey information.
2. Shared learning.
3. History.

Analytical Information

Analytical information (sales, share, customer satisfaction, and profit/loss) should be a requirement both nationally and regionally. Information companies make data in most categories available in either raw or managed formats. You have more of a chance of getting by without data on a national basis because your base and risk is spread so widely that if you throw out the highs and the lows, your decisions usually still remain in a moderate comfort zone. In regional marketing, however, you are oftentimes dealing with very specific strategies and tactics that need to be managed and evaluated with accurate information. Regionally, you don't have as much room to spread out your risk; therefore, the more tools and resources that you have available, the better your chances of developing a successful program.

The previously mentioned regional marketing budget should appropriately handle the cost of information. Later, I discuss understanding your competition and turf, focusing on appropriate versus inappropriate information subject to competitor's sales and share. Other appropriate pieces of information are customer/account profiles, socio-economic/demographic data, and regional economic trend reports.

Shared Learning Information

Shared learning information is a data source that is easy for us to control yet, more often than not, underutilized. By shared learning, I mean the experiences (good and bad) of people currently doing the job. When I was a regional marketing manager, I had counterparts in the South and in the Western U.S. regions. The central part of the country was left as a control region and not staffed with a regional marketing manager.

Since we were so busy inventing the regional marketing wheel, we rarely discussed what was working or not working with our individual programs. In fact, on several occasions, we learned that we were developing similar programs on parallel paths, and we had no awareness of what the other was doing. This lack of shared learning information can result from being too preoccupied with problems and frustrations, as well as not wanting to share programs due to a perceived feeling of competition among the managers. Both of these barriers to communication can be reduced or erased by having communication/fact-finding/show-and-tell sessions legislated by management as an ongoing process within the development of the regional marketing system.

Internal Competition

Don't underestimate the notion of competition among regional marketing managers, especially if these regional marketing managers are your lead people to develop the program for the organization. Usually these types have been well selected and have been successful within the company. These people are typically highly competitive. Unless you deal very early in the training program with the need for teaming and bonding by these individuals, you will have virtually no information sharing or synergy between these pioneers.

Chronicling the History

Chronicling the history is essential, not just nationally but regionally as well. Because general office/headquarters types have program analysis as part of their culture, national analysis is usually not a problem. The more you decentralize the marketing and sales function, the more you need an analysis system in place, because, routinely, this is an element of the business cycle that is left out. Decentralized managers usually are in "today forward" modes regarding the business. This is true because most of the field managers are from the sales discipline, and *generally* speaking, the sales discipline does not have as an active part of its culture an emphasis on analysis or "rear-view mirror" management. Systems may be in place, but the utilization of those historical information systems is often somewhat lacking.

Please Analyze!

The more regional marketers analyze the programs they have conducted, the better off they will be from a future-quality basis. If a program has been successful, then a quick, timely analysis is a good piece of public relations for regional marketing at large, but, more importantly, a vital element if the program is run for a second year. This post-program analysis (or post-mortem if the program was a failure) is absolutely vital, especially if the regional marketer is less than fully empowered regarding programming budget. Frequently, regional marketers, even with a fully funded budget, need assistance from product groups and/or general sales management to execute all of their desired programs. If a second-year program is being considered then the regional marketing manager and/or the brand groups ought to table the request (either for concurrence or money or both) until a competent analysis of the year-one effort has been conducted.

The assembly of information, the sharing of common learning, and the development of program history are three vital elements of a successful regional marketing program. These inputs, coupled with instincts and an understanding of general conditions, will almost always insure that at least by year two of any effort, you can make competent and well-founded program decisions.

TIMING/LOCATION PRINCIPLES

Timing

Timing and location are merged because they are logistics principles. If you are developing a regional marketing program and have some flexibility, it is incumbent to manage the principle of timing in a proactive way. Many companies go through an annual budget development process that takes quite a bit of time and analysis. The budget meeting process usually takes several weeks. These meetings usually occur several months before the beginning of the next fiscal year. Since the majority of the rough-draft work on programs and budgeting is taking place at this time, it is wise to have the regional marketing manager on board either a little before or coincident with this process. To have this person join in after the new fiscal year budget and programming are determined creates a very frustrating circumstance. This situation is not only frustrating for the regional marketing manager but is frustrating for all the audiences that touch this manager. The manager is put in the awkward position of developing programs without legitimate funding and then having to sell those programs internally to attract financial support. These sales are usually very difficult because they are usually sales against a budget reserve that is much smaller than the already committed funds for rough-draft programs.

This issue of timing is very real and should be managed if the opportunity exists. If this can't be proactively managed, then upper management needs to revise its expectations of the results and programs of the first-year regional marketing manager.

Location

Location is a principle about which I have personally changed my mind. While it seemed blindly obvious that regional marketing managers ought to be in the regions and not in the general office of the company, I, for the first year and a half, disagreed with this approach, principally because I did not have a hands-on budget. Therefore, I found myself constantly selling the system to try to procure funding for my programs. This would have been much easier if I worked in the "bank" (the general office). I further believed that as regional marketing was being developed, it should not evolve into *totally* decentralized marketing. This decentralized situation makes it very difficult for vendors of the company to approach the whole organization with good ideas. When vendors (suppliers) sell to large decentralized companies, they are sometimes forced to make 5 to 20 different presentations to try to interest all the different market decision makers. Thus, many good programs are lost or never presented because of the logistics of selling to a decentralized marketing organization.

Now I believe that regional marketers *should* geographically live within the region that they are responsible for. To make this location decision functional, they should have a real budget and a strong shared learning system developed.

As I discuss later in Section 4, Ultimate Regional Marketing, I believe that the need for market intimacy is more important now than it ever has been before. As we move toward regional brand/product strategies and customer-ized marketing (wherein we line up with the customers' needs and wants and develop programs), we have to be physically closer.

Critically, if regional marketing managers can develop good, solid regional programs and spend less time trying to sell existing general office systems, then field-located regional marketing works. If the environment that exists in your company's regional marketing effort does not lend itself to a strong empowerment situation, then you should initially manage your risk by having regional marketers located in the general office to ensure that the early stages of the regional marketing effort is done well.

SUMMARY

The general principles of regional marketing that have been discussed do have a priority to them. Undoubtedly, the most important principles are the combination of empowerment, recruitment, and training. If these three principles are in place, then your program probably will succeed even if you don't manage the issues of information, shared learning, analysis, timing, and location well. Of course, I believe that ultimately all of these general principles should be integrated into a well-balanced, straightforward effort.

Understanding these general principles and coming to comfortable grip with them should make the principles within the marketing mix elements of pricing, advertising, merchandising, promotion, and product much easier to implement and understand.

SUMMARY CHECKLIST

1. *Are your regional marketing managers empowered? Are they blessed by upper management? Do they have specific budget authority? Are they placed within an appropriate level in the organization to be able to interact with decision makers?*

2. *Have you recruited your people carefully? If your focus is primarily customer-driven, do these folks have a strong sales background? If*

your strategy is principally targeted toward the consumer, do these managers have a strong marketing background?

3. *Have your people engaged in a reasonable training program before engaging the position? Have you utilized the practice of cross-training? Have you kept your training sessions small? (I really believe in this!) Do you have an ongoing training program in place?*

4. *Have you provided your managers with the needed analytical information? Have you established a shared learning system? Do your managers truly understand that for the long-term needs of their jobs they must be "part-time historians"?*

5. *Have you given any thought to the timing of staffing the position? Will they be in place with enough time to understand the business and impact on next fiscal year's planning? Will you place your regional marketing managers in the central office or in field positions? If you deploy them in the field, will they immediately report to their location, or will they stay in the central office for a period of time?*

6. *To whom will the regional marketing managers report? Will they be involved in matrix-management?*

7. *How will they be evaluated and rewarded?*

Chapter Five

Regional Promotion Principles

INTRODUCTION

If there is an element of the marketing mix that seems to be accelerating in the area of regional marketing, it is promotion. The never-ending search to smartly regionalize promotion seems to be equivalent to the quest for developing the perfect mousetrap. The packaged goods, airline, automotive, fast-food industries, as well as others, are plunging headfirst into the arena of regional promotion with mixed results.

This race to the promotion trough is being fueled not only by companies' infatuation with promotion, but by the emergence of promotion departments within advertising agencies, radio stations, and their customers.

One type of promotion is couponing. The consumer packaged-goods business has for a long time experienced coupon proliferation. Open up any Sunday paper and you will undoubtedly see hundreds of various coupon offers. While coupons are by most definitions a form of promotion, other promotions such as free trips, magazine subscriptions, special events, contributions to the local school/park/athletic team, and even the Daughters of the American Revolution are becoming watered down and suffering from saturation. Although this sounds somewhat cynical on the topic of promotion, it is a fact that well-principled promotion can be a valuable regional marketing and national tactic.

TWO TYPES OF PROMOTION

Promotion should be addressed from two perspectives: first of all, promotion that is targeted to the ultimate end user (consumer) of the product or service; second, promotion that is targeted toward the channel of distribution, also known as the trade or customer.

The area of consumer promotion that encompasses coupons, refund offers, and frequent buyer/flyer type programs have really expanded in recent years and perhaps even leveled off and started to mature.

Trade promotion has many forms, but it is basically incentive-driven. It provides something extra to the channel of distribution to help you sell your goods or services. An example of a trade promotion might be giving away free tickets to a local sporting event. The sales representative might give away 100 tickets to XYZ customer. That customer (say, a local grocery chain or video store) would in turn give the tickets away to their employees or possibly raffle them to consumers. In exchange for the tickets, the seller would expect preferential treatment for their product. In the case of the video store, perhaps the seller would request that a poster of a certain movie be hung in the front window for a period of time. At the grocery store, perhaps a display of the seller's product would be requested.

Trade promotion, while employed for years by food brokers and direct store delivery organizations (I might add, very effectively), has not been executed with finesse by the majority of manufacturers. The type of promotion targeted toward the trade, however, is receiving new attention. One only has to explore employment opportunities in the sales and marketing field to find that companies are either developing from scratch or enhancing their trade promotion departments.

EIGHT CONSUMER AND TRADE PROMOTION PRINCIPLES

1. Keep the Promotion Simple (It Doesn't Have to be Perfect)

When it comes to promotion, it is really easy to make it difficult, and sometimes difficult to make it easy! Human nature (which, sadly, becomes corporate culture) tries to complicate even the most simple and clean activities. The topic of promotion by its very title attracts very creative people. Everybody, it seems, wants to be a promoter. It's as though somebody once told all creative types that the more complicated and involved a promotion is, the better it will perform. This statement cannot be farther from the truth.

I'll never forget an experience I had a couple of years ago. I flew into one of our district sales offices to review a promotion that two very creative and well-regarded salespeople developed. These talented folks had not received any training on regional marketing at all, and I was curious to see what they wanted to do. These two salespeople were very excited about stepping out of their discipline and into the marketing arena. The promotion they presented me had every conceivable promotional twist to it. In a marketing sense, it was the equivalent of the Star Wars Defense Initiative. This promotion was targeted toward a joint relationship with a local amusement park. By itself, that was a very sound promotional alliance. However, the program broke down because of its complexity. Their plan called for the following elements:

1. Twenty five cents-off coupon in seven local newspapers.
2. In-ad refund for trade circular publications.
3. Special mention on the packaging of participating brands.
4. In-packing a coupon for the theme park in specially marked packages of participating brands.
5. Free amusement park tickets for distribution by local retailers.

6. Multiple purchase incentive for discount admission.

7. Local radio announcement of the event.

8. Free product giveaway to the first 100 people.

9. Event sampling of product.

10. Possible T-shirt giveaway at the local amusement park.

11. Hospitality and function area set aside for key guests.

Almost any two or three of these elements combined would have created a successful promotion, but this promotion as presented was very cumbersome and had no chance of being successful. The projected costs far outweighed the potential benefits. As proposed, this plan would have taken a legion of marketers to develop and execute.

2. Each Local Promotion Must Have a Local Owner

Even though I fear the concept of decentralization when it comes to regional marketing, I do believe that if a local promotion is decided upon, then a local person must supervise it. A local promotion, if it's part of a larger network of promotions, can be *managed* from another city, but it should not be *executed* in absentia. Having a person on-site and intimate with the promotion will enhance success.

Procter & Gamble's Food and Beverage Division has been very involved in special event and promotion management. One of the most expensive and potentially rewarding promotions that we have been involved with was a sponsorship of the Ringling Brothers and Barnum & Bailey Circus. This circus, which appears in approximately 90 different markets over the course of a year, had very widespread national implications, but it was still a promotion that could be tailored to a regional market. We had a wide range of business results behind the circus from "best promotion ever" status to "abysmal." Review and analysis of the promotion determined that a common denominator in almost every market where the promotion worked was a local coordinator. We also found that if people could take themselves conceptually and intellectually from being a coordinator to being a manager, then the promotion improved that much more.

On the flip side, where we had no real dedicated local circus manager, the promotion generally underperformed. Further, we found that the attitude of the coordinator/manager was critically important. If the coordinators truly believed that they were owners, then strong results were forthcoming.

Again, a local owner on any program is very important, but make sure that the person is a *true* owner and manager and not a custodian of the program.

3. The Event Is Not the Event; the Event Is the Result

Local promotions, especially special event promotions, can hypnotize and distract good sales and marketing types. Before you undertake any promotion or event, determine your true business objectives. In most cases, the local event takes place to help a local sales force sell incremental business—that is, sell more computers, cars, burgers, or boxes of cereal than would have been sold with a national promotion. If the primary purposes are business results and increased sales and awareness, then work as hard as possible and be strategically smart so that results can be delivered.

When I worked with special events at Procter & Gamble, we became involved in a program called unlimited hydroplane racing. Generally, this program was executed very well and provided for a few years of strong business results. However, in some markets the local sales management lost touch with the program's true purpose. Instead, they believed that while selling incremental product was nice, the primary purpose should be customer relations . . . Trade schmoozing for lack of a better word.

Frankly, I have no trouble with that being the objective of a promotion (or special event); sellers can always benefit from social time with customers. However, the hydroplane program was sold to marketing management as a way to increase the sales organization's ability to sell incremental product. If, as a by-product, customer relations were improved, then great;

however, customer relations should *not* have been the target purpose of that promotion at the expense of sales.

Beverage companies such as PepsiCo, The Coca-Cola Company, Anheuser-Busch, and Miller Brewing Company are masters of local promotion management. I have spoken with several people at these companies who agree that it is crucial to hold to the principle of the event being the result! If the event becomes larger than life and no business result is forthcoming, then the event should cease.

If improved customer relations is your business objective, identify it up front and manage to that point. If your business objective is public relations and/or a cause related to charity, then define it up front and manage to that end. If increased sales is your business objective, then quantify it, manage it, and measure it. If your business objective is increased brand and corporate awareness, then spend and invest strongly in that direction.

All of the results—customer relations, public relations, increased sales, and brand awareness—are noble and appropriate subject to a product's needs and a market's opportunity. Figure out your objective and clearly communicate it to your people. Don't change the rules of the game by shifting from public relations to increased sales volume if your sales numbers are weak.

4. Be True to a Product's Strategy

An effective regional marketing manager knows the stategies of the products the company sells. If product strategies are known, then good regional marketing managers won't do stupid and incongruent things on behalf of products. Along with product strategies must come a clear understanding of that product's target consumer. For example, a regional marketing manager should not try to develop a promotional relationship between Jif peanut butter and the local annual tractor pull. (Jif's target consumer generally won't be at tractor pulls.) Praise, however, goes to the person who develops a long-term promotional relationship between Jif peanut butter and elementary school systems; Jif peanut butter targets young moms. Jif can try to influence their purchase of Jif peanut butter by a program that offers money (subject to the amount of Jif purchased) to the *local* parent-teacher associations. This is a national promotional concept that is applied with regional value.

5. Avoid Promotion Layering (most of the time)

Promotion layering occurs when you have two different and distinct promotions occurring within a market at the same time on the same product. Generally, this redundancy creates a certain level of confusion and is very hard to analyze in a post-promotion manner. Simply stated, it's hard to determine what worked!

Layering often happens when the national marketing plan is agreed to with long lead times, and then a local promotion opportunity occurs on a short lead time. (I have, however, had the reverse happen.)

Usually, there is an overwhelming temptation to disregard the issue of lead time and try somehow to find a way to execute the local promotion, even though it will be layered on top of an already strong existing national promotion.

While the short-term consequence of layering is usually a slightly stronger business lift than if either promotion had run by itself, this is a short-term way to look at regional marketing. There are two reasons why this is generally wrong to do: (1) Every promotion that is executed should be analyzed and evaluated. When you have two promotions running concurrently, targeted to the same product or product group, it is very difficult to identify which promotion stimulated the most business. Since we are typically in a business for the long haul, we really want to understand what works and should avoid this phenomenon of layering. (2) The cost of two simultaneous promotions usually does not return a justifiable business lift and creates a situation of diminishing returns.

However, as much as I just warned against promotion layering, it is appropriate to acknowledge that occasionally promotional layering can be complementary if well thought out with appropriate lead time. The following are a few examples of when promotion layering within a particular marketplace can be effective:

a. When the national promotion does not adequately cover a market. This happens occasionally when companies use coupons, radio, billboard, print, and television programs. Often, it is cost-prohibitive to buy time on enough different radio stations to completely cover a marketing area. When this happens, part of the market goes promotion naked. If an opportunity exists to develop a simple, easy promotion to cover the unmarketed area, then there is no redundancy. Theoretically, you can have two promotions going on in the same defined market, but because of gaps in coverage, the promotions can be compatible.

b. When you develop an overall marketing plan, you typically try to market as efficiently to the largest group of consumers as possible. Sometimes when you do this, you exclude very large sub-segments of a market, such as blacks, Hispanics, people of Jewish faith, etc. It is not uncommon for companies to run promotions targeting the Christmas time period, but also supplementing those Christmas promotions with Jewish-targeted marketing that recognizes Hanukkah. Since Christmas and Hanukkah generally have close promotional timing, in heavily Jewish markets you can conceivably have two promotions occurring on the same timing but targeted to different consumers. This is especially important in markets such as New York City and Miami where a very large percent of households are Jewish.

c. On occasion, you will find that special events and holidays overlap: for example, Easter and the Boston Marathon. When these generally one-of-a-kind timing coincidences occur, it is appropriate to explore linking Easter and the Boston Marathon. These situations should not be totally dismissed because of the possible phenomenon of layering. Instead, you might be able to develop a huge promotion.

Another example of this situation occurs when, nationally, you have contracted to be involved in large programs such as Ice Capades, Barnum & Bailey Circus, concerts, or multi-date/

multi-city type events. In this case, you will have circumstances that will certainly create layering with the national promotion plan. You can either consciously allow the layering to occur, or you can substitute. Substitution of one event for the other is a practical way of financially justifying a product's investment in a particular market during a particular time. All that has to be done in this case is that the national program, say, a national back-to-school promotion targeted to appear in September, can occur in all markets nationally except where the circus is visiting. The fair share of that market's portion of the national promotion expense can be used to help fund the special event.

A final thought on layering: Don't confuse layering with an integrated marketing effort using the various elements of the marketing mix (promotion, advertising, pricing, and product). It is very common to run ongoing advertising, run promotions, and execute some kind of pricing strategy—at the same time. All of these variables working together create great synergy and can be very beneficial, providing each element has a strategic purpose.

6. Make Promotions Proactive Not Reactive
This speaks to the issue of lead time! Good local promotional opportunities really do abound. If you understand your company and the systems that exist to facilitate regional marketing efforts, then one of the elements of the system will be a recognition of needed lead time. Nothing is more counterproductive and frustrating than identifying a good local opportunity and not having enough lead time for implementation.

It is essential that you manage the issue of appropriate lead time, or else you can give regional marketing a bad name within your company, with your customers, and with the consumer.

7. The Proverbial Payout Syndrome
The proverbial payout syndrome is defined as the promotion generating enough incremental sales at least to pay for the cost of the promotion. This is a principle that I struggle with. I

believe that local promotions should be able to justify their existence in many ways, such as finances, goodwill, and awareness. On the other hand, I also believe that we should focus on long-term results whenever possible. Herein sometimes resides a conflict. This conflict also stems back to the general regional marketing principle of empowerment. If regional marketing programs are not paid for by the regional marketing manager, but instead are funded by a central marketing office appropriation, then generally speaking the attitude that prevails is that it had better work in the short term, or there is no chance it will be around for the long term. This norm prevailed at most of the companies I researched regarding funding local events. What is unfair within this system is that a lot of programs realistically need more than one year to financially pay out. Year one is when you gain the experience and maturity to have a successful event for years to come.

I'll never forget a promotion that I worked on in New York City targeting inner-city blacks. The event was an extremely successful one with black customers and black consumers, and sold enough product to be a financial success during year one for four of the five participating brands. The other brand happened to be Crisco shortening, and the extra cases sold almost covered the investment by the brand. There were a variety of reasons why the results were not better, and I believed we could attend to those shortcomings during year two of the program. However, I humbly submit that I could not make the sale to the Crisco shortening marketing group. The event to them did not pay out during the initial year, and they did not renew involvement for year two.

There are two ways to look at whether a promotion pays its way; they are financial payout and intestinal payout:

Financial Payout. This term refers to whether the extra sales from the regional effort generated enough total profit to cover the cost of the event. Let me assure you, there are more than enough issues built into this seemingly innocent description than I can outline in the limits of this chapter. Instead, let's explore briefly one example and accompanying issues.

Example: The local automobile dealers in a region are thinking about announcing a promotion in which for the month of November, everyone who test drives a particular car will be entered into a drawing for an all-expense-paid vacation for two to Hawaii. The promotion will be announced around October 15, and the drawing will take place on December 1. The promotion will be announced via radio on stations at times when their target consumer will be listening. The total cost of $25,000 will cover radio, a discounted cost of the trip, and all miscellaneous expenses, such as drawing tickets and announcement posters. The region dealers will cosponsor the event with a local travel agency; in return, the travel agency will receive mentions in the radio announcements.

The dealers know that after the promotion, when all related costs of selling this vehicle are in, there is about $2,500 available per this type of car to invest in marketing. Again, this $2,500 is predicated on the car not being sold at a giveaway discount. Therefore, the intent of this promotion should not be selling on a price-related basis; instead, quality of car and the interest this promotion creates should substitute for price discounting. It quickly appears that the region dealers need only sell 10 *incremental* automobiles to break even and cover the marketing investment (cost of promotion). Also, please remember that this $2,500 worth of marketing investment per car assumes that the car is priced to deliver reasonable internal profit. The marketing investment is called the marketing dollars available.

The region dealers have established that 10 cars need to be sold to justify this expense. The general managers should then look at their base period, which was sales last November and their ongoing sales track. This reveals how many of these types of automobiles they have been selling every month for the last year. Then, the dealers need to look at internal variables, such as consumer interest rates this November versus last November and what the overall industry forecast holds for sales for the next six months to a year. As well, the dealers have to take into consideration whether or not it is near the beginning or the end of the fiscal year. Lastly, the needs of the dealerships and their short-term and long-term strategies need to be addressed. The dealers may be in a terrible profit crunch and might want to turn that $2,500 of budgeted marketing expense into profit. This need might call for a cancellation of the promotion if the promotion was not deemed strong enough. On the other hand, if the promotion is evaluated as having significant strength and could be a strong boost to overall sales, then the promotion could help with overall sales volume and profit.

National Hypothetical

Another form of financial analysis relative to regional promotion is a calculation that national companies should recognize as national hypothetical. (National hypothetical means the cost for one market is simply multiplied by the number of markets the company has.) Let's use the automobile example already mentioned. Perhaps this is the type of promotion that the central product marketing group for a major domestic automobile company wants to encourage through its dealer network. The company knows that by working with the local dealers previously mentioned, the cost per dealership is about $25,000. (We should assume that dealers in a particular area [region] will group together to make the promotion more cost-efficient.) Suppose the company has 50 regions nationally; therefore, $25,000 times 50 would translate into an overall promotion cost of $1,250,000 for this program to be run nationally. Since the company's central office has been involved in national marketing promotions for some time, they have an idea of what is appropriate relative to promotional costs and estimated benefits of a promotion. If $1,250,000 is appropriate, then it passes the national hypothetical test.

It is important to recognize that the national hypothetical cost for any promotion is just a barometer, which should only be used as a guideline relative to reasonableness. National hypothetical cost should not serve as a veto instrument. If a local opportunity exists that could have huge regional payout, it should be pursued. Regional promotional opportunities usually cost more money than a national hypothetical model; however, in certain markets the regional returns can be several-fold higher than the nationally projected (hypothetical) results.

Intestinal Payout. While financial payout is an objective method of evaluation, intestinal payout is subjective. This payout does not have a mathematical calculation behind it; Instead, it is subject to feelings about a promotion.

Intestinal or gut instinct has to come into play because too often we get bogged down reviewing the short-term financial projections instead of looking at the long-term regional opportunity. Regional marketing for many companies is akin to breaking new ground. When you do this, of course there are risks, but the rewards can be substantial. Earlier in this chapter, I mentioned an inner-city black program I was involved with and the fact that the Crisco shortening brand did not agree to participate for a second year. My instincts told me that Crisco shortening should have been involved because one of the primary reasons we had problems during year one of the event was pricing. I couldn't say that our pricing situations would be corrected because I was asking for an appropriation of money months before the actual promotion was to take place. Since the amount of money requested was low, the risk was not very great. Again, I couldn't make the sale to the brand group, and from a financial point of view I can't blame them. However, business decisions are most often not automatic, and a combination of financial and intestinal payout considerations should take place to manage risk. Regional marketing events, as well as national promotion plans, need a blend of financial and intestinal review. I think the financial analysis of a decision should outweigh the gut feeling. However, marketing and salespeople need some leeway within the system to manage with their instincts.

8. Post Promotion Analysis

Post-promotion analysis is a principle that most marketers adhere to religiously and most salespeople ignore. This principle is critical to regional marketing, especially if the marketer has to get money for programs from product groups or a central office. Essentially, you want to audit what worked and what didn't. By recognizing this principle as separate and distinct from the others, you will insure a multidimensional overview of the promotion. This principle combined with the seven previous principles should serve as a well-balanced outline to analyze promotions.

SUMMARY

It is easier to fail than to succeed when it comes to regional promotion. This chapter reviews eight principles that should serve to help you manage promotion risk. While all of these principles have just about the same strategic weight to them, two do stand out. The first principle, keep the promotion simple, should be religiously followed. This is hard to do because we naturally want to add value to our work but unknowingly often over-complicate our programs. The second principle, each local promotion must have an owner, is critical. You can have all of the other seven principles working reasonably well but if ownership is lacking then there is a reasonable probability of poor results.

SUMMARY CHECKLIST

1. *Was the promotion kept simple and easy to execute?*
2. *Did the promotion have a local owner? How did the owner do?*
3. *Did the promotion meet its intended objectives?*
4. *Was the promotion strategically aligned for products involved?*
5. *Did the promotion avoid layering? If layering occurred, was it strategically and tactically aligned?*
6. *Was the promotion proactive with good solid lead times in place?*
7. *Did the promotion pay out? If not during this year, does it have potential to financially succeed during the next execution? Did it pay out intestinally?*
8. *Applying the post-promotion analysis, was the promotion successful?*

Chapter Six

Regional Pricing Principles

INTRODUCTION

Pricing is what I call the anxiety principle. Pricing is one of the most extreme and overt tactics a company can use. Further, if you don't price your product correctly on a price-benefits-competitive basis, you could be in trouble.

When a company chooses to take a price increase on a product, usually their competitors (in moderating degrees) publicly slander the action but privately applaud it. A company's reducing its pricing is usually an aggressor tactic, which can create a short-term competitive skirmish or a long-term death spiral. It may also be a reflection of lower raw materials costs, superior manufacturing capabilities, or more cost-effective competitive infrastructure. As one who has been involved in literally hundreds of pricing actions, I attest that when you use pricing as a tactical weapon in regional or national marketing, you had better subscribe to various principles. National pricing moves are relatively easy and usually confined to changes in list prices. List prices are the base prices (unpromoted) that a company charges a retailer for a good or service. Pricing really becomes difficult when it is done on a regional basis. Correctly doing regional pricing is a marketing art form. Regional pricing management is usually done under duress and is generally neither a salesperson's nor a marketer's first tactical choice. Most national sales management types want pricing done as simply (no geographic differences) as possible, so that their sales forces are not distracted. They are also fearful of developing different regional pricing that has customers in one region buying a good or service at a significantly different price than customers in another bordering region. This lack of pricing equilibrium confuses consumers. Consumers can't (or don't want to) understand why a hotel room in downtown Chicago costs more than one in downtown Roanoke, Virginia. Most marketers would also rather use advertising and promotion instead of reduced price to sell product.

PULL VERSUS PUSH

There are two general strategies in selling that are greatly affected by pricing. One is "pull" strategy, the other is "push." Ideally, most companies would much rather create pull-marketing strategies. Pull marketing occurs when the consumer demand for a product is so strong that the seller does not have to offer incentives (usually reduced price) to help the product sell. One of the best recent examples of pull marketing is the Mazda Miata. The Miata is a good product, well researched to determine the consumers' desires, and also advertised strongly. The price of the Miata was generally not an issue; in fact, because of high demand and low availability, consumers were actually willing to pay above the sticker price. Mazda did not have to be aggressive and play a pricing game with this product, and they had a very successful introduction. Consumers were literally pulling the car out of dealerships because of good-product concept and advertising. This situation is the opposite of Mazda having to discount the car and push it toward consumers. Mazda Miata, along with Trivial Pursuit and the Cabbage Patch doll, are good examples of successful pull marketing.

Most products, during introduction or sometime during their lifetime, need to be price discounted and engaged in some push strategies. Pushing occurs for a couple of reasons. For example, when companies are under short-term pressure to increase sales numbers, they discount. Sometimes when product inventories build up, costing money and disrupting cash flows, companies reduce the product's selling price. Other times, push pricing strategies are used if a company blatantly wants to go on the offensive against a competitor and own a certain selling period. Just take a trip to any supermarket a few weeks before Halloween. You will see the world's candy companies going nose to nose, price point to price point against each other in very aggressive ways in hopes of enhancing sales volume and capturing market share. The price points will be sharp and sometimes predatory, but because simultaneously there is also a strong in-store (point-of-purchase) effort under way, the price will still provide a small profit for the retailer. You will also see an incredible shifting of gears going in the candy category once Halloween is over and retailers have overbought. What you usually see is a fire sale with retailers having trouble giving seasonal candy away. The product is often sold below cost, with no pull activity going on like advertising or in-store merchandising.

As Benjamin Franklin once said, "If you fail to plan, you plan to fail." When it comes to pricing, you must first start with principles and develop a strategy. Without good planning, principles, and strategy, your tactics could be very misguided.

ELEVEN REGIONAL PRICING PRINCIPLES

1. Offensive or Defensive?

Generally determine whether your product will have an offensive or defensive pricing posture. In other words, are you going to be a pricing leader or follower within a particular region? Offensive pricing strategies do not necessarily mean being the first to discount. Offensive pricers can be the first to take price increases to recover increased cost from raw materials or to improve profit margins. As a manufacturer, you do not really control retail pricing; your customer does. However, you heavily influence retail pricing by how you treat (the management of) the price you charge the retailer for your product. You also need to know the pricing principles of your customers.

The offensive pricing leader can also announce to customers its intention to hold, drop, or increase prices. This action gives competition a chance to pick up pricing information from customers or the press, and then they have the opportunity to follow the leader. This kind of offensive strategy appears in the announcement of manufacturer rebates on automobiles and other equipment, as well as announcing via the press that a particular airline is planning on escalating or de-escalating ticket prices by a certain percent during a coming season. In the consumer goods industry, manufacturers often identify the net cost of a product before the product can actually be bought by the retailer. This is necessary because retailers usually plan their advertising and merchandising programs several weeks in advance. This announcement usually creates a swirl of competitive price reacting. Manufacturers must be very careful in this area because announcing prices too far in advance may be misunderstood as price signaling.

2. Who Is Your Pricing Competition? Make the Choice
Most business arenas have more than two or three key players vying for market share and sales. Because of a variety of factors, competing brands have different brand shares or business development in each market. Because of multiple competition and different market development and characteristics, it is not an optimum business situation to have standard pricing.

A regional marketer must decide who the true regional competition is. National brands with different market strengths and regional brands that can be powerhouses in some markets and not exist in others really add a degree of difficulty in the regional pricing decision-making matrix. If you don't decide who your true pricing competitor is, then you will end up pricing against every competitor. When you price against all competition, you become very inefficient. Your pricing dollars are spread thin, and you don't usually get these dollars reflected through to the consumer in the way of optimum reduced retail pricing. Alternately, if you are chasing two competitors' pricing and one discounts their prices one month, and the other discounts prices the next month, you become discounted for both months. When you are discounting all the time to the consumer, it is hard to determine your valid ongoing everyday price. You can create the impression that you can only be sold on discount, and you lose sales when you increase your resale price to normal levels.

3. Product Equity—It's Not an Unlimited Checkbook

A product can spend a lot of time trying to develop a positive impression among consumers. This positive impression is called product equity. Reducing the price for a prolonged period of time on a product that the consumer believes is of high quality and deserves a price premium can become a nightmare. This concept of brand equity should be managed delicately. Occasionally, you can withdraw equity (decrease the price) for short periods of time, but be very careful not to change the consumer's perception of the appropriate long-term price of the product. The recognition of regional product perception differences is critical. If a product has high equity in the Southeast and little to no equity in the West, it would be callous to discount the price nationally to enhance sales velocity in the West. Your reduced price investment is probably mismanagement and fiscal irresponsibility for your southeast territory, yet this frequently happens.

BMW has addressed pricing in that they have developed various tiers for their cars. The 300 series, 500 series, and 700 series provide consumers with somewhat different BMW products at different price levels. This is all done without eroding brand equity of the BMW. It also allows BMW to regionally promote and price with greater flexibility. This tier concept is a much smarter approach than just having the 500 series and playing with the price regionally. In fact, BMW, because of this tier system, periodically advertises finance and lease incentives on their 300 series to make them more competitive with other products based upon regional sales performance and competitive marketing. Offering finance and lease incentives may seem un-BMW-like, but it is regionally smart and does not damage BMW's image.

The Duncan Hines brownie product group also recognized the need for tiers a few years ago. They found themselves competing with two different tiers (types) of Betty Crocker and Pillsbury brownies. One tier was a very basic low-price belly-stuffer product. Another tier, in which Duncan Hines had a leading position and significant product equity and strength, was the pricier value-added brownie segment. Since Duncan Hines did not have a product entry in this low-priced tier, they found themselves continually discounting their value-added product. This was very successful for the short term, but the more the consumer saw Duncan Hines brownie discounted, the more they waited for the price to be reduced for purchasing. The brand equity was eroding, and the product group decided to come out with a Duncan Hines entry in the lower-priced tier and maintain their presence in the higher-priced tier.

Today, Duncan Hines, as well as Betty Crocker and Pillsbury, has products in this lower-priced tier where they can do price discounting and be generally competitive with one another. Brands in this tier are called fighter brands because they generally have a cost structure that will allow reasonable price-fighting to take place. All three companies also still maintain product in the higher-priced tier, and there is generally less price discounting going on. This scenario provides improved profit balance for the three manufacturers and good profit for the retailer. The consumer also sees a reasonably fair price on brownies.

4. Manage the Price Spread

This principle of price-spread management is, in many ways, directly related to regional product equity. All products are not perceived by customers and consumers the same in every region. Additionally, all products do not have the same brand strength (equity) in all regions. Therefore, price spreads, or what I call consumer-tolerance levels, exist for almost all brands.

Specifically, a price spread is the difference between the price the consumer sees for your product and the price the consumer sees for competitive products. Some products might need a lower price than that of the competition in some regions, and they might be able to stand a higher price in other regions. This difference is usually attributable to consumers' perception of the price-benefit relationship and the brand equity that a product has. As mentioned earlier though, a consumer will choose to switch brands at some point. When a large portion of your consumers start to leave your product because of improper competitive pricing, you have, in effect, priced yourself beyond the pricing threshold and mismanaged the price spread.

Acceptable price spreads usually don't expand or constrict unless there is significant product news, strong advertising copy, or a particular competitor goes out of business or goes through some kind of a dramatic change.

Understanding regional price spreads on your product and then managing the price spread issue is an important regional pricing principle.

5. Understand Absolute Regional Pricing
If, as a regional marketing manager, you have a large territory, there is a very real possibility that some of your markets will have significantly different absolute prices for your products. This is usually a function of the pricing styles of your customers. If your region happens to be the eastern United States, then it is very conceivable that your product in Portland, Maine, will be priced at a significant difference than your product in Baltimore, Maryland. Don't let this difference concern you. Just make sure you manage the very important price-spread issue relative to your competition.

6. Be Faithful to Your Internal Margin Needs
While you are evaluating price spreads and absolute regional pricing, keep one other important principle in mind: be faithful

to your internal margin needs. Too often companies determine what they believe would be a healthy internal margin requirement for their products and then abandon this principle subject to three factors. These three factors are (1) the need for more profit (perhaps to shore up other faltering products), (2) reaction to competition, (3) testing "how high is up" and pricing to what the market will maximally bear.

When you depart from your agreed to internal margin and take the price up to return a greater profit, you should be extremely careful. You can get lulled into a false serenity that could over time have a very negative backlash from both your customer and consumer. When your pricing is out of line for whatever reason, it usually takes a lot more spending for advertising, promotion and public relations than the offsetting price increase that resulted in the pricing problem.

Don't misunderstand me on this point. It is normal to have to take the price of goods and services up (and sometimes down). The real issue here is *why* you are taking the price up. If you have had a product improvement that will deliver greater value and had some investment cost to get that improvement, then clearly it is acceptable to "cost to recover." If the general market price for raw materials that contribute to both you and your competition's cost go up, then you probably have a reciprocal increase. Customers and consumers generally understand this occurrence. When you increase for some of my previously mentioned reasons, then beware.

Price, volume, and profit are intricately interwoven. They often defy the law of physics that states, "for every action there is an equal and opposite reaction". When your price-volume-profit relationship is out of balance because of unprincipled profit expansion, you can really adversely effect volume and you will not have ". . . an equal and opposite reaction."

7. Always Build-in a Pricing Reserve
The cost of national and regional pricing tactics can sometimes be hard to predict. Using price as a tactic is as close to marketing warfare as you can get. A few years ago when the odds of

conflict with the Soviet Union were much greater than they are now, a pricing guru friend of mine gave me some advice that I will never forget. He said, "If you are going to attack the Soviet Union, don't run out of gas in front of the Kremlin!" He really meant, if you are going to take offensive pricing action, make sure that you hold back some money in reserve in case of a counterattack. This reserve is the difference between whether you have pricing stamina or not. Major pricing initiatives don't usually work just in the fiscal quarter in which they are initiated. You sometimes need to maintain your activity for several quarters. This takes stamina, conviction, and a well-planned initial strategy. This reserve money can either be used to fulfill the needs of a contingency plan, be turned back to the product group as profit, or reinvested in subsequent pricing actions.

8. Legally and Ethically Let Competition Know What You Are Doing

This principle does not mean collusion or any kind of unethical or illegal pricing discussions among competitors. Instead, when you take pricing action, make sure that you notify your customers quickly and simply, giving no room for misunderstanding the specifics of the pricing tactic or the overall business intention. If your customer then wants to alert your competition, you can't control that variable. In fact, typically, that is a normal reaction in some industries. The accurate understanding of specific pricing and business objectives can prevent problems. The worst thing that can happen is for a product-pricing decision to be announced and the competition to misread or misunderstand it and react in a completely unnecessary way. I have seen this happen many times because, legally and ethically, competitors can't speak to each other in the area of pricing. Therefore it is incumbent that whatever pricing action you take, you do it in as clean and ethical a manner as possible.

The concept of "mailbox" should be understood and used to ethically manage the principle of letting your competition know your pricing intentions. A mailbox account is an account that has told you they believe in letting your competition know exactly what you are doing and vice versa. Identifying mailbox accounts is extremely helpful in avoiding misunderstanding and thus in short-circuiting chaos.

9. Understand Pricing Boundaries

If you choose to discount a product in the Southeast that has national distribution, be aware that you could be creating an uneven selling situation if that product gets diverted out of the Southeast and shows up in the Midwest. This issue of diverting is common to many industries. While there are ways to reduce the pain of diverting, this circumstance really does get in the way of clean regional pricing.

10. Post-Pricing Analysis

Did your pricing activity produce the desired results for your business or product? What did competition do? If you recognize and chart general market conditions and competitors' responses to your pricing moves, you can develop a forecast. You can generally learn much by mapping the actions/reactions of competitors and what the customers and consumers do relative to pricing. The use of post-pricing analysis enhances the quality of future pricing decisions.

11. Have a Central Pricing Coordinator

If you are a large company with several products and multiple regions, you must find a way to manage the potential stress and confusion. A way to do this is by having either a central pricing coordinator or category pricing staff. This function will serve to add continuity to your pricing plan. It will also provide for a checks and balances mechanism in the system, between central and decentralized sales personnel.

SUMMARY

Because pricing is extremely important to the overall marketing mix, national pricing on all brands all the time is very unrealistic. A regional marketer needs principled and ethical regional pricing to effectively be able to have a balanced regional marketing program.

Unlike other chapters, you must integrate *all* of the regional pricing principles into a solid effort. The only value that you must uphold at all costs is that you maintain an honest approach to pricing. All of your decisions and actions must be done legally with an unflinching commitment to fairness for all customers.

SUMMARY CHECKLIST

1. *Are you going to adopt an offensive or a defensive pricing strategy?*
2. *Have you determined your primary pricing competition? Have you developed systems to collect pricing information?*
3. *Do you understand that by continual discount pricing, you are eroding product equity?*
4. *Do you understand the price spread (either favorable or unfavorable) of your product compared to the competition's?*
5. *If you have multiple markets within your responsibility, do you understand the absolute pricing differences?*
6. *Are you faithful to your internal margin needs? If you increase or decrease your price, is it for the right reason?*
7. *Do you have a pricing reserve built into your strategy? Are you prepared for an even stronger competitive pricing reaction, or have you put all of your "eggs in one basket"?*
8. *Are you careful to conduct all your pricing moves within a legal and ethical framework? Are you keeping your pricing tactics simple and easy to understand for both the competition and yourself?*
9. *Do you have a clear understanding of your various pricing boundaries?*
10. *Do you always review the impact and ramifications of your pricing activities after the fact?*
11. *Have you selected a central pricing coordinator?*

Chapter Seven

Regional Advertising Principles

INTRODUCTION

Of the primary marketing mix elements (pricing, promotion, advertising, and product), advertising is the toughest to measure and to assign value, but is potentially the strongest business developer of them all.

I characterize myself primarily as a salesperson who understands and utilizes marketing, rather than a marketer who understands and utilizes sales. With that as background, I have sometimes been accused by my sales peers of being related to the traitor Benedict Arnold. This uneasiness (although most of it with good humor) comes from my belief that good advertising programs should be deployed as regional tactics whenever possible. In fact, when thinking long term, I usually opt for advertising and product tactics over pricing and promotion tactics.

I particularly like advertising in general (if it's *good* advertising), because it creates consumer demand, which, as mentioned in a previous chapter, becomes a pull synergy. Good advertising enhances product image and can deliver both short- and long-term results. Good advertising can make impressions on many more people than the other three elements combined. Advertising should be viewed as the train engine that on the front end of any product's life creates trial and awareness. As the product grows and matures, advertising allows the product to contemporize. In essence, it provides for graceful aging or is sometimes the fountain of youth. Oftentimes during the course of the train's journey, it needs to be supported by an engine bringing up the rear, which helps push the train and helps the advertising engine. This is somewhat of a convoluted analogy, but if you can visualize the train with the engine being advertising, pulling the cargo (the product), and a backup engine coming behind the train (usually price discounting), you will understand the concept of pull and push synergies.

Frequently, advertising misfiring is a result of management's (both agency and client) blind pursuit of efficiency and ignorance of regional differences. How else can you explain the following recent national radio copy campaign? A major import car company ran some well-done national radio spots about how a particular feature of the car significantly aided its performance in ice and snow. The timing was right—February. However, this should have been a regional execution so that consumers in Southern California would not have heard it!

Advertising is an extremely tough business. Having been involved in pricing, promotion, advertising, and product decisions, I can unequivocally say that advertising decisions are the toughest. I disagree with most people regarding the quality of advertising today. Most people I've spoken with, whether it was for interviews for this book or just conversationally at large, believe that the quality of advertising has fallen off and that advertising mediums are dominated by below-average efforts.

In contrast, I believe that most advertising is good, but that advertising clutter creates too much distraction; then, because of advertising saturation, most of the advertising becomes somewhat homogeneous. It is frequently of reasonable quality so the "bar" has been raised, and it is tough to produce a distinguishable effort. Regionalizing advertising is a very distinguishing tactic.

REGIONAL ADVERTISING IS GROWING

Historically, the majority of advertising dollars have been spent in what I would call conventional mass advertising ways. Specifically, the bulk of the advertising investment dollars have gone toward national television and national magazines. There is, however, a steady transition going on. That transition is marked by a shifting of advertising dollars away from national and towards regional executions. I strongly endorse this advertising dollar migration from national to regional because, ultimately, advertising needs to be more balanced. I recognize the need for national "cookie-cutter" campaigns because of their overwhelming efficiency. On the other hand, regional differences are so extreme relative to demographics and product preferences that national programs are sometimes incredibly inefficient. The word *inefficient* is usually reserved for regional programs rather than national programs because of increased development and executional time and cost that regional advertising sometimes demands. However, running a national television program that might be reasonably identified by 50 percent of all consumers and totally unknown to the balance of your viewers is a severe misfire. Usually, the people who are not impacted by the national advertising message can be identified as being in a certain region or of a certain ethnic group. Special attention should be given to this large pocket of potential consumers with some kind of regionally adjusted advertising.

A good example of this refocus can be illustrated by understanding Crisco shortening's advertising. Earlier, I was unflattering toward the Crisco brand regarding promotion. This time, however, I will applaud. Crisco shortening originally ran national copy that was clearly focused towards the South and the "frying experience." The advertising focused specifically on frying chicken and utilized a country music, as well as Southern special-events, type focus. This advertising strategy was mediocre. The Crisco shortening brand was well developed in the South and did its principle business in the South. The advertising was on target to help hold that business but was off target to

Northern consumers. The Crisco shortening brand recognized this and wanted to build its business in the North while holding its business in the South. To do this, the brand group and advertising agency developed a regional advertising focus. They maintained the frying-experience approach in the South and developed a new baking-experience focus (principally pie baking) for the North, where Crisco shortening was being used much more for baking than for frying.

The Crisco shortening advertising example is one that years ago would never have been executed. It would have been deemed inefficient because of having to develop two different types of copy and having to execute two different regional media plans. Fortunately, now it is viewed as inefficient to alienate a large percentage of consumers with irrelevant, off-target advertising.

Regional advertising can and should become more important in the future. The more advertising becomes regionalized (and stays affordable), the more likely it will be that advertising will make a positive contribution to the marketing mix and justify its investment.

I believe that everything starts with principles and then expands. The same is true with regional advertising. For regional advertising to have maximum benefits, various principles should be followed.

THREE REGIONAL ADVERTISING PRINCIPLES

1. Choose Your Weapons Wisely
This principle relates directly to your choosing a regional advertising medium correctly. Most large national companies believe that regional advertising is accomplished by adjusting the blend between national network television advertising and local spot television advertising. Since there is usually no change or regionalization of the actual commercial, companies feel pretty good about this. While I am somewhat critical of defining this as regional advertising in a true sense of the word, I suggest that

this is certainly a step in the right direction. The real strength in this quasi-regional advertising approach is that if companies pick the right local television station, then pick the right time for airing their commercials, they can strongly improve the probability of delivering their commercial to their target listener.

The concept of choosing your advertising weapon, however, goes much deeper than having a national advertiser adjust the balance between national and local television usage. Instead, advertisers should look carefully at other local advertising mediums. Some of the best local mediums to explore are radio, print, billboards, and a medium I call "all other". Let's look at these four types of advertising delivery systems.

Radio. I am tempted to say that radio is the most versatile regional medium that exists. By *versatile*, I mean you can identify the right station and the right air time to target your primary consumer. Subject to the strength of the radio station's signal, you can reach more people than with all other mediums, except television and possibly magazines. Giving an advertiser a common forum to integrate advertising and promotion is another versatile trait this medium exhibits. This is difficult for television to do. A print medium can integrate advertising and promotion, but with less impact.

Impact is a key word and another aspect of radio's versatility. Radio is alive. People hear it; it has action. Radio and television breathe and have life. Radio, although it can be costly in absolute terms, is often undervalued from an advertising point of view. *Undervalued* should be defined as receiving more advertising than you actually paid for. When it comes to radio, the upside of incremental advertising (above and beyond what you paid for) is unparalleled by any of the other mediums.

A specific example of getting more than you paid for via radio occurred during a program I was involved with behind one of my brands. We spent approximately $3 million for a radio program in some key U.S. markets. We paid various rates for various amounts of advertising in each market. Upon auditing the execution of the program, we found that not only did the radio stations run the agreed-upon amount of actual advertising copy, but the disc jockeys (or air talent) went beyond what they were required to do and say. Specifically, we found that disc jockeys in their normal dialogue were also talking about our product. Often, the disc jockeys had to announce promotional spots regarding the product and would actually have to read advertising spots. In several cases, the disc jockeys made additional comments to the script for the promotion or the advertisement of that product. Of course, sometimes there is a concern about product ad libs, but generally speaking, there is very little downside risk because disc jockeys do not want to offend the stations that employ them. In the final analysis of this joint promotion and advertising program, we determined that we received approximately 20 percent more advertising impact than we paid for.

When reviewing advertising as a medium, you need to review the radio station's ratings and listener profile. If a particular radio station lines up well with your target consumer and is billing out at a reasonable cost, then radio should be considered as a medium.

Print Advertising. Print advertising comes in many varieties: advertising in newspapers, regional/national magazines, school yearbooks, local retail circulars, and direct mail. If you choose to use the print medium, then you need to completely understand which print medium is the right one for you.

Print, although not as versatile and alive as the broadcast mediums of television and radio, is still very strategic. Print advertising is generally less costly in an absolute dollar sense than most mediums and has a stranglehold (in a positive sense) on the consumer for some business categories. Examples of print bastions are in the areas of real estate, automotive sales, grocery sales, and retailing. It is believed that more automobiles and real estate can be sold through print than through any other mediums.

Another benefit of print is its ability to deliver detail. Frankly, I view this benefit as an oxymoron. I don't generally think that any advertising or promotional message should have high levels of detail. Advertising and communication to the consumer need to be kept as simple and clean as possible. However, print advertisement can deliver script/product message/promotional detail that also can be enhanced by a visual.

Since advertising is basically a format to trigger initial interest or awareness, print can usually provide an advertiser with practical follow-up material such as an address to write to or, more importantly, a phone number to call. Other mediums try to do this, but sometimes pencil and paper are not within a consumer's immediate grasp, and a broadcast message usually sneaks by them. To prove my point, how many times have you wished you had pencil and paper handy to pick up an address or a phone number of some broadcast message and just couldn't do it. In contrast, print vehicles have already done this work for you and in many ways should be considered more user friendly. Print forums also help when you have to communicate directions or price on a regional basis.

Billboards. In many ways billboards should be considered print advertising. Billboarding as a concept can occur much closer to the ultimate point of consumer purchase by actually penetrating inside retail outlets. Big posters of product beauty-shots are often on display above meat counters, produce sections, car dealer showrooms, fastfood counters, airline terminals, and even doctor and dentist offices.

Billboarding also occurs subconsciously at the point of purchase. Just remember the painting that Andy Warhol did of the Campbell's soup cans. This type of billboarding (solid in store brand fronts) is incredibly powerful and can act like a magnet to draw consumers to the ultimate point of purchase.

Outdoor billboards also have tremendous advertising potential. The key word here is *potential*, for I believe that billboards generally are not optimally used. This occurrence is primarily not the fault of the billboard agencies. Instead, it is more a result of the traditional advertiser not thinking regionally. A billboard's primary value is its location—it is, in essence, real estate!

Billboards can be a powerful advertising tool when used correctly. The correct usage of billboards happens when you

- Understand traffic flow around the billboard and vicinity of the billboard and general demographics of the people viewing this board.
- Provide a simple next-step on the board. It may be an 800 phone number, an airline destination, or a street address with directions for a fastfood restaurant.

    Phone numbers can come in handy during traffic jams, and directions to a fastfood restaurant are useful if the restaurant is close to the billboard.
- Advertise related items on the same board. A good example is one company's peanut butter and another company's jelly. A stronger execution would be aligning with the customer. A good example of this is a national brand peanut butter on the same billboard with a supermarket's private label bread. This gives good exposure to the national brand and the store's own product. This alliance, an effort paid for basically by the peanut butter manufacturer, not only results in strong related item advertising but could also materialize into promotional merchandising by the retail customer on behalf of peanut butter. When those kinds of relationships occur, you have achieved the pinnacle of regional advertising—advertising that also communicates promotion.

Billboards are a valuable item in the regional advertising tool box.

"Other Mediums". There are a host of other regional advertising forums subject to your type of business. These forums range from advertising at sports stadiums, special-events-type sponsorship, in-store electronic and point-of-purchase mechanisms, and radical types of inflatable advertising.

My mission is not to discredit these other types of unique regional advertising efforts because these advertising vehicles can work very well. However, test the different regional advertising mediums and understand that they all have their own unique sets of executional systems; then, pick the top one or two best types for your business.

The name of this principle is "choose your weapon wisely." It is important to research which weapon is right for you. Don't rush into regional advertising, because your first effort must be sound. Traditional mass media/national advertisers sometimes approach regional efforts initially with "tongue in cheek." In regional advertising, try to reconcile the difference between efficient and effective. Regional advertising is not as efficient from a cost and executional framework, but it may be a more effective business influence. Lastly, keep the execution simple, well targeted, and compatible with your marketing strategy in that particular region.

2. Identify and Cash in on Regional Value
While related to the previous principle "choose your weapon wisely," this principle has more specific responsibility. When you choose your weapon, *you* are picking a style of communication. When you identify regional value, you are deciding *what* to align with regionally.

It is important for advertisers to realize which advertising mediums, special events, regional characteristics, and regional causes have value. Recognizing this principle forces regional advertisers to make choices about what regional variables or differences have value. It is the chore of a regional advertiser to pick the "hook" that will catch the most fish. That hook may be particular publications or particular radio stations. The hook, in a broader sense, may be leveraging a local event (like Mardi Gras in New Orleans) or recognizing strong regional issues, such as extreme sensitivity to the environment in the Pacific Northwest and the New England states.

Perhaps Kevin Scully, advertising director for *Yankee Magazine*, expressed it best. *Yankee*, which has been in print for 56 years, is read principally by either displaced or actual Northeasterners. Kevin stressed that

Yankee has invested 56 years in understanding and coddling our consumer to the ultimate degree. We love our subscribers, and we have an intimate relationship with them. *Yankee Magazine* has value! We may not be able to help you sell a lot of your product in Arizona, but if you want to sell more product in the Northeast, then hop on. We at *Yankee* have been building up credits and trust with our consumer for years. When you buy advertising in *Yankee* [providing your product lines up well with *Yankee's* reader], then you are receiving a return on the 56 years of our investment. Of course, this return will cost you advertising dollars, but if your consumer and our reader are one in the same, then your advertising investment should reap rewards.

Kevin went on to indicate that well-placed regional advertising should by its very nature (because it is more targeted and customized) provide companies with competitive advertising advantages. He explained that the buying public can be fickle, but one thing they do seem to overwhelmingly react to is being addressed personally. In an advertising sense, the consumer is addressed personally when spoken to regionally. People do remember it when they are driving to work in Cincinnati and see a huge billboard saying, "Thanks, Cincinnati, for making Pepsi-Cola number one."

A hook does not have to be a particular publication or radio station. It can also be the leveraging of geographic characteristics. A good example of this is the Absolut Vodka campaign. The worldwide advertising agency, TBWA, depicts the Absolut Vodka bottle shape using different formats. A great execution was the print advertisement entitled Absolut Manhattan. The ad transformed the actual Central Park area of Manhattan from a green square patch to a green patch in the form of a bottle. This ad regionally identified well with the huge New York metro upscale market. It was also generally believed that Absolut Vodka consumers would recognize this clever transformation of Central Park regardless of where they lived in the United States. In essence, they ran a regional print execution targeting New York that, because it leveraged Central Park, had national awareness value. Just in case this belief didn't quite hold true in Los Angeles, they ran a similar campaign/print ad entitled Absolut LA, which depicted a print ad that featured a swimming pool scene that attempted to evidence LA life-styles. Of course, the pool was in the shape of an Absolut bottle.

3. Regional Testimonial—The Ultimate Weapon

This principle is a combination of principles one and two and integrates using the right weapon (medium) with regional value. The Nutri-System Weight Loss Program has launched a very powerful campaign, using radio as their primary weapon. Nutri-System determined that the real hook (value) to the radio listener was the disc jockey. They targeted lead radio stations in several major markets; then they made customers first out of local disc jockeys who needed some weight-loss control. This created some tremendous endorsements, which in the final result became regional testimonials. Not only were the disc jockeys doing their job by announcing the commercial spot, but they became highly believable with strong translatable sales results by actually being part of the commercial. As with the radio example mentioned earlier, the Nutri-System program received much more value and air time than they paid for.

While the types of linkages that Nutri-System pursued may seem logical, they are not always easy to achieve. Again, the difficulty arises because national/traditional advertisers suffer from paradigms and sometimes just can't let go on behalf of regional efforts. Intellectually, the national advertising agencies and their clients agree with regional advertising, but they are concerned about the executional complications and possible increased costs.

I spoke with a combination of 10 advertising agency executives and their clients. I posed to them the following question: If you wanted to run a testimonial campaign for a product endorsement, would you try to recruit one strong national spokesperson or five different regionally strong people? Nine out of ten opted for the one strong national spokesperson; yet interestingly, eight out of the ten thought that the business results would be stronger if they went with the five regional spokesperson approach. The primary reason for not choosing the regional approach was the perceived executional complexity of coordinating this type of program versus one program and one spokesperson.

This type of advertising scatoma (blind spot) exists broadly. On a positive note, I do see some companies trying to use this regional advertising opportunity. Of particular note are Nike, Reebok, and Marriott. A recent Nike execution features Michael Jordan. This copy flashes regional landmarks and the names of some key U.S. cities and talks about the Nike product and Michael Jordan's exploits in those cities. This is good regionalized treatment of a national program. Nike also uses regional billboard programs featuring local sports celebrities. Reebok's Pump sneaker has a commercial that features basketball stars from different teams and cities in very short vignettes on the product.

Marriott Hotels has made the ultimate structural regional advertising decision—they consciously segment their national and regional advertising efforts. Nationally, Marriott conducts an overall advertising campaign that really addresses the image of Marriott and its dedication to customer satisfaction and service. The national advertising presents the quality of Marriott as a product, giving a positive at-large impression not only of Marriott but also of the lodging industry. This campaign is conducted by a national agency, but then it allows regional advertising agencies to line up with a regional Marriott business section. Denny Bond, General Manager of the St. Louis Marriott Pavilion, explains:

> All of the Marriott properties benefit from national advertising that is coordinated by the Marriott corporate group. However, since regional management involved with the local hotel properties strongly believes in regional advertising, we have the flexibility to align with local advertising agencies and public relations companies. These agencies are much more plugged in to our needs and can help us with better regionally targeted advertisement.
>
> The national agency for Marriott selects the regional advertising agencies with our input. This is important in that the Marriott message must be consistent even though there are regional

demographic differences. The Marriott central office also wants to make sure that the regional advertising companies are of good quality and align well with Marriott's national effort. It is programs like regional advertising that allow the local hotel to become the St. Louis Marriott Hotel versus the Marriott Hotel in St. Louis. This may seem like a subtle difference to a person outside of the Marriott culture; however, it is critical to our integration into whatever community we are in, and regional advertising certainly helps make that happen.

SUMMARY

As advertisers and their agencies know, it is fairly typical when a product's business results are suffering that advertising dollars are pulled and shifted into other shorter-term marketing tactics. This is usually done because advertisers generally have a hard time quantifying business results delivered behind advertising. For advertising to truly work, it should get closer to the consumer, and one way to do this is through regional advertising. The more an agency and an advertiser align with the value of regional advertising, the better their pull (advertising) business results will be.

For this to happen, traditionalist mass advertiser clients will have to concede a bit more. Simultaneously, advertising agencies should push a little bit more for regional efforts and expand their capacity to help make this happen. Advertising agencies nationally and internationally are coming more and more to the realization that they need to become more full-service. I believe that full-service is not defined only as having an expanded promotional capability, but becoming competent in pricing and product programs as well. This ability to become better *general* business operators, as well as expert advertisers, increases the respect clients have for them.

If this is to happen, agencies will have to take the lead and, if they are smart, they will invest resources in owning the understanding of regional consumer differences. Understanding your consumer and the various media options and utilizing regional hooks in a sound cost/benefits way transforms the agency from an executor/consultant to a partner.

SUMMARY CHECKLIST

1. *Do you know what is available regionally in your advertising toolbox? Are you comfortable with your understanding of the various advertising delivery systems relative to your product need and target market?*

2. *Do you know good regional value when you see it? Beyond the appropriate delivery systems, what/who are the regional hooks?*

3. *Once you've identified the hooks and the mediums, can you bring it all together in a usable format? Do you utilize a combination of national/regional agencies to help translate and customize your regional advertising message?*

Marketing Assessment Process (MAP)

T his section focuses on five primary concepts:

1. Understanding your competition.
2. Understanding your customer.
3. Understanding your consumer.
4. Understanding yourself.
5. Understanding your turf.

These five groups of understandings provide a strong framework to determine the probability of success of your regional or national marketing plan. While these concepts have broad application, they are particularly important when developing regional marketing strategies.

To execute regional programming correctly, you need to be a bit smarter and more focused. The word *regional* implies that you are dealing with either a segment or a sub-segment of a larger marketplace. When you evaluate national marketing plans, typically you can throw out the highs and the lows to come up with an overall summary of results. Marketing to a bigger piece of geography and volume can sometimes allow you to get somewhat lazy and stale. However when you bring your programming right down to a specific market with a specific program, possibly even focused against a specific customer, it is quite necessary to integrate all five of these understandings. If you do this, you can manage your risk and best achieve your full potential.

SUN TZU

Not many original ideas are occurring in the areas of marketing and sales today. By following the aforementioned marketing assessment process, I thought I had discovered something. As I conducted research for this book, much to my dismay, I found a veritable business genius who had discovered a couple of these focuses some 2,500 years ago.

The person I am referring to was the very successful soldier Sun Tzu who fought in China during the sixth century B.C.! The following nugget was offered by Sun Tzu as he spoke about the enemy and himself. All that has to be done to the following quote to make it relevant in today's business environment is to change the word *enemy* to *competition*:

> Know the enemy and know yourself, and in a hundred battles you will never be defeated. If you know only yourself, not the enemy, your chances of winning and losing are equal. If you are ignorant of either the enemy or yourself, you will surely be defeated in every battle.[1]

Too many companies today are consistent with the latter part of Sun Tzu's quote:

---

[1] General Tao Hanzhang, *Sun Tzu's Art of War: The Modern Chinese Interpretation* (New York: Sterling Publishing Co., Inc., 1987), p. 51.

If you are ignorant of either the enemy or yourself, you will surely be defeated in every battle.

Hopefully, this section will provide ways for you not only to get in touch with yourself and the competition, but also with the customer, consumer, and your turf!

Chapter Eight

Understanding Your Competition

INTRODUCTION

Business today is a series of "what if" questions. While the most frequently asked "what if" question is usually targeted to customer and consumer reactions, the second most popular "what if" question focuses on the competition. How many times have you said, "What will my competition do if I drop my price?" or, "What if I introduce a new product next year? How will my competition react?"

Understanding the competition should be a core business prerequisite for managers. While competitive understanding is very important to managers, it should also be a shared responsibility with the rank-and-file people of a business organization. Since a lot of competitive understanding comes from pure data collection, the importance of competitive information should permeate all levels of the company. Competitive information data collecting should be rewarded and recognized as integral to the company's future business existence.

Once a company makes the decision to understand the competition, it is important to move forward in one of two ways.

UNDERSTANDING THE COMPETITION AS A BALANCED APPROACH

Understanding your competition is just one of many ways to nationally and regionally advance the business. A competitive understanding integrated with knowledge about the customer, consumer, yourself, and the turf should give you more options to manage your business. Basically, this is the focus of Section III.

UNDERSTANDING THE COMPETITION AS A PRIMARY APPROACH

Generally, the focus of your strategic business planning is targeted against the competition versus the other understandings. In a sense, all the other focuses subordinate themselves to an intimate understanding of the competition. *Generally*, this is an incorrect way to address the business environment. This type of business concentration usually yields to over-intellectualizing competitors' impacts on your business plans. Additionally, and most importantly, this preoccupation usually breeds defensive/reactive strategies and tactics. This is not always wrong, but it can lead to business decision-making paralysis and, in an absolute sense, late decision making.

An example of this paralysis often comes in the area of product pricing. I have engaged in both sides of the pricing equation and, in effect, have been both the paralyzer and the paralyzee!

Specifically, when we have chosen to have a totally reactive/defensive pricing posture on a product, we are usually held hostage by our inability to *ethically understand* competition's pricing initiatives. Over time, competition should be able to chart this reactive pricing tendency and gain the upper hand. An advantage can be gained by understanding what our customers' lead time requirements are regarding pricing decisions in their stores. Once we understand customer requirements, and once we understand that competition is reactive, then the trap can be set. Winning the pricing battle with these under-standings in place becomes much easier. The offensive pricing company merely waits until the last minute, then delivers pricing information to the customer. A competitive company (that is, reactive/defensive) takes time to collect this information, process it, and develop a competitive pricing response. By the time this process takes place, the company may be too late to respond. The offensive/well-timed company will win the pricing game for the near term. There are several ways to defend against this tactic, one of which is to have regional marketing managers who are empowered to make decisions on pricing. This regional manager needs to be trained as to the brand's budget and regional strategies and also needs to have a pricing reserve budget available. If quick, well-educated decisions can be made by trained regional people, then the competitive response processing time is shortened greatly. If the company also has good competitive information collection systems in place, a pricing response can come immediately on top of the competitor pricing communication.

This is somewhat troublesome to large national companies because regional pricing is tricky. A safeguard that should be maintained is a central pricing coordinator, not a committee, but one person who can comprehend the impact of how changing the price or promotion of a product in California affects the business in Arizona.

Preoccupation with the competition can *sometimes* be the correct overall business direction. This happens when through understanding the competition, you believe that your competitor is doing just about everything right. If you then understand yourself and know you will not be able to achieve a product technology breakthrough or do not have a deeper advertising, promotion, or pricing pocket, then you choose a follow-your-competition strategy. What you hope will happen is that the competitor you are modeling will look at your approach with disdain and a level of arrogance. Once they cease to respect you, and you in essence are employing a copycat strategy, you are 50 percent of your way to long-term success. This strategy may take a long time to pay out, and it may take some personal ego-swallowing, but I have seen success over time by companies having a total focus on the competition, because frankly they knew the competition was doing almost everything right.

Over the last 10 years, I have seen this strategy work in the very intense competitive environment of grocery retailing. Some grocery chains have ignored the standard grocery retail preachings of find your niche versus competition and exploiting it. Instead, these retailers made the conscious decision not to be niche operators, and they invested in understanding the competition. Then, they recognized humbly that the competition was doing it better than they were and followed the leader. Of course, the long-term strategy of following the leader is eventually to catch and pass the leader!

HOW TO UNDERSTAND THE COMPETITION

Understanding the competition is not the easiest task to engage in, but it is not impossible. The following principles, strategies, and tactics should help decrease the frustration of this focus and enhance the quality of competitive information received and the decisions driven by this information.

1. You Must Define and Distinguish between Primary and Secondary Competitors

The *primary competitor* should be defined by the following statement: If I only have the resources (product, pricing, personnel) to compete with one competitor in the market, who should that be? An addendum to this question should be: What are my chances of success, and how long will it take to prevail? Specifically, which competitor do you believe you have the ways and means to target and the highest probability of success against.

Secondary competitors are competitors that *must* be recognized and tracked because they could have significant effect on your business (especially regional). The size and strength of your company will really dictate whether or not you react to a secondary competitor.

Defining the competition is the most important step in understanding the competition. As a regional marketing manager, I had great difficulty trying to manage the battle on all fronts. For a short period of time, I tried to engage all competitors, all the time, anyplace I could in both offensive and defensive strategies. The lack of focus as to who was the primary regional competitor (with a recognition of secondary competitors) was overextending my personal capacity and was marginally impacting incremental business results.

A primary criticism of regional marketing is that it can be too complex and confusing. To those critics, I offer a resounding **You're right—if you don't reconcile which way to aim.** Marketing at large and regional marketing, specifically, are a series of strategic choices. Sometimes in making strategic decisions, it is tougher to decide what not to do than what to do. Unless you decide who your *real* competition is, you will overtax your resources. A saying that should remind you of your inefficiency is "to do everything is to do nothing." This idea is discussed more in Chapter 11.

Once you decide regionally who your primary competitor is, take aim! Also, dig in, especially if nationally your brand decides that their primary competition is different than yours. I experienced this with Jif peanut butter. We had very effective national strategies with well-defined primary competitors. This national plan worked well in all of my markets except two. I lobbied for over one year to adjust the strategy in these two markets to address the regionally different primary competitors. Once the change was made, we moved to number one share in one market and number two in the other. We did it over a two-year period, without throwing money at the markets.

2. Be Your Competition

There is a saying, "If you can't beat them, join them!" While I don't literally go that far, I suggest that you do everything ethically short of that to ultimately understand the brands and the corporate culture of competition.

Many businesses are managed by teams now. I recommend that a business team have as one of its principal focuses an understanding of the primary competitor. A person on the team should become a competition specialist. Over time, this should have significant value to the business unit or brand.

There are several ways for you to *be* your competition. It is important here to note that to *be* the competition does take time. Being the competition is also more a state of mind and an understanding of general behavior, culture, and business systems of the company. This is different than the actual process of gathering specific brand or company intelligence to help perfect advertising, promotion, product, or pricing. The ultimate objective of being your competition should be to think like your competition.

Being the competition takes hard work and a couple of focuses:

- Buy and use the competitive product(s). If it is a service, then obtain the service. Become totally familiar with the product or service you are competing with. View this relationship first as a consumer, then as a competitor. Try to dissect the product or service and then hand it over to conventional experts. Try to gain understandings in their core business disciplines such as finance, product supply, advertising, sales, and so on. Ask finance people in your company to try to understand your competitor's accounting structure. Do they evenly assign overheads to all the products, or do they shift overheads to make some of their businesses more competitive? Ask product supply people to understand how much integrity their supply system really has. Contact customers to understand if they have a conscientious channel of distribution and if they really believe in customer service. Talk to your advertising agency to best understand how the other product is advertised. Attend consumer focus groups and listen to people and their impressions about the companies' products.
- Visit the city where the headquarters is located. If the company is a big company and influences the city, try to understand that. Subscribe and read the local newspapers. Oftentimes, local newspapers glean information on acquisitions and new product initiatives before the national media.

You may find this absurd, but notice what kinds of people the company employs. Most companies are either not making a commitment to diversity or are slow in the process. Show me a company that is only paying lip service to the issue of diversity, and I'll show you a company that has every right to worry about the future. In fact, I annually attend a reception that a magazine has for its advertisers. The magazine is supported by traditional manufacturers and retailers from all industries. I pay special attention to the industry that I work in and the competitive advertisers. One company, a direct competitor, has been making significant strides regionally over the last five years. It may or may not be a coincidence, but the people from that company who attend this magazine's annual reception have dramatically changed from a nondiverse to a well-balanced, diverse group in the past five years. I have noticed that over the course of these years the attitudes of this company have improved from the contact I had with their people. I don't engage in direct business discussions, but I can tell by being around them that they are more comfortable as a group, less intimidated and less myopic!

While it is important to understand the attitudes and cultures of your competition, it is equally important to understand business details. To that end, Sam Walton founder of Wal-Mart has the right attitude. He periodically visits competitors' stores with a group of his managers. They tour the store to notice what one thing they think the competitor is doing right. They are not charged to focus on what the competition is doing wrong.

3. Gathering Intelligence

People outside of my business often laugh when they come to my office and see a strange piece of equipment in a common work space area. When they ask me what the equipment is, I tell them that it is a paper shredder. People's conventional thinking is that paper shredders belong only in foreign embassies and the Pentagon, but I assure them that while somebody who breaks into our office is not really going to threaten national security, he or she certainly can damage our best business interest.

While I am well aware of unscrupulous methods of gathering information (my company and I personally have been victimized before), I will refrain from discussing them in detail in this book. It is enough to say that not all the planes flying over our production facilities have been on sightseeing tours, nor have the phone calls from alleged college students wanting to know about a new product introduction been legitimate.

It has been reported that if you have a basic understanding of physics, an aptitude for engineering, and accessibility to any major college library, you can build a nuclear weapon, provided you can access the materials. My point here is that most information is available through perfectly legitimate and ethical means. Several legitimate sources of valuable information exist:

A Company's Annual Report. I know that an annual report of a competing company is not going to make or break how well I sell my next year's marketing plan. However, if a company is multisectored and has several businesses, then usually the annual report gives a top-line review of those individual businesses. In a broad sense, it helps me understand whether or not the business unit that I compete with is winning or losing! Are they in the 7th straight year of losses, or are they in the 15th straight year of contributing to the overall company's profit picture? Has a new general manager for the business unit been appointed in the last fiscal year, and is that new manager a domestic or international manager? Can you find out if the old manager was promoted, retired, fired, or left the company? Who are the new board-of-directors members for the year, and whom have they replaced? Is the upper echelon of leadership becoming more diverse or staying the same? As I review the annual report's financial statements, how is the company doing, and what does their management predict for the future?

Third Party Reports/Articles. In the automotive industry, just take a look at J.D. Powers reports. You can learn much about customer/consumer satisfaction in one quick review. Take a look at a Nielsen report and you will quickly find in it market share, pricing, volume, and merchandising on a regional basis for manufacturers in the consumer package-goods business in hundreds of categories. Pick up a *Consumer Report* now and then or one of the major sales and marketing magazines. These sources tell a great deal about new products and failing products. Some of these industry magazines, along with magazines like *Business Week, Newsweek,* and *Time,* are enlightening in areas of sales restructuring and company marketing advances. Many times, as a sales manager, I learned about a new product a competitor was introducing from magazines like *Advertising Age* and *Advertising News.* These magazines sometimes provide broad product information about a new item six months before it comes to the market.

You also acquire information by reviewing recent patent applications as well as reviewing material from trade mark registrations. When a company wants to name a new brand, they must publicize the name to see if any challenge will take place to the name.

Attend Regional Trade Functions. Companies have differing attitudes about attending regional trade functions. My general comment is don't let your own company's constipation get in the way of spending some time with competitors and customers. Early in my career, I stayed away from gatherings such as these, but now frequent them as much as is practical. Again, if one of my objectives is to understand the competition, what better way to understand the competition and possibly gain insights into their business directions than to be in the same physical environment. When attending these functions I do not hope or expect to understand what a competitive product's next promotional program will be. Instead, I like to see if a company's regional management is staying constant or in transition. Often at these functions, I listen in amazement to program speakers from the competition as they brilliantly outline their business plans and focuses for the coming year. I've also learned much about companies' attitudes regarding special events, the environment, packaging, trade relations, promotion, and category management.

4. Catalog History

It is vital to have a tracking system on competition. The areas that should be tracked are pricing, promotion, merchandising, new initiatives, and special events. Track what they do in these areas relative to proactive and reactive measures within your market. If you don't do this now, then you should start doing it from "today forward." Once you develop accurate history, you will have very clear insight into the future. The history should become revealing enough for you to forecast competitive behavior.

5. Map the Territory

We will discuss this under the principle of understanding your turf later on in this section. However, to make sense of everything that has been discussed in this chapter and to "bring it home" regionally, a clear map needs to be developed to understand your competitor's regions and trading areas.

SUMMARY

Doesn't wanting to understand your competition make sense? It never ceases to amaze me that the Oakland Athletics baseball team is being regarded as the quintessential organization for understanding the competition!

My intention is not to belittle the Athletics; rather, it is to scold the people that are so impressed. What the Oakland Athletics baseball organization does with their in-depth use of statistics and tendency modeling should not be amazing; it should be normal. The Athletics own an intimate knowledge of competitors, obtained by very public and ethical ways.

Business is not getting easier. It's getting tougher, and companies need to take advantage of every ethical way possible to survive and advance themselves. Understanding your competition should become a way of life, especially if you intend to evolve from a national marketing strategy to a regional marketing strategy.

SUMMARY CHECKLIST

1. *Have you decided who your primary and secondary competitors are? Do you have systems in place that track both of these competitor levels?*

2. *Do you have somebody on your team who can "role play" the competition?*

3. *Have you made the collection of competitive information habitual? Do you know how to gain competitive knowledge about competitors?*

4. *Have you developed an historical tracking system so that you understand the previous actions/reactions of competition relative to all aspects of the marketing mix?*

5. *Have you developed a map which identifies your competitors' marketing zones?*

Chapter Nine

Understanding Your Customer

INTRODUCTION

Understanding and getting much closer to the customer is one of the strongest business directions of today and for the future. An individual or company that doesn't wake up to the "rightness" of customer understanding and customer service will lose personally and professionally.

Historically, companies have always been too focused on improving market share and chasing volume at the end of the fiscal year. This blind pursuit of market share and volume in the absence of a long-term vision has easily cost companies billions of dollars in inefficiencies. Additionally, the hunt for share and volume has created short-term chaos and strained customer and vendor relations. A shifting from short-term pursuits to long-term plans with a recognition that profitable volume is necessary to fuel any strategic change is paramount. If a company can couple this with a passion for customer satisfaction, then they have a more healthy and winning approach.

If you have a happier and more satisfied customer (assuming no real business aberrations), then the business should expand in both volume and market share. Objectives must be set, but only if a corporate vision focusing on customer understanding and satisfaction is in place.

CUSTOMER VERSUS CONSUMER

For the purpose of this chapter's discussion, the customer is the person or company being directly sold to. That seems like a simple concept, because a lot of selling is through channels of distribution. Specifically, at the two consumer-goods companies I've worked for, a customer was not the consumer; the customer was the supermarket, drug store, and mass merchandiser executive or buyer. When Pepsi-Cola sells its programs, it sells first through a bottler/distributor network (some it owns; some are independent), so the distributor, not the consumer, is the first customer. These customer relationships prevail in most product business frameworks. Service industries often sell directly to the consumer.

In the late 1980s and early 1990s, much was written about companies like Procter & Gamble and Rubbermaid Incorporated. These companies were given significant credit for really listening, understanding, and trying to foster a positive business relationship with the customer. This recognition is very deserved because these companies and others recognize the value of teaming.

TEAMING

One of the key ways to begin to improve customer relationships is through teaming. Many articles on customer teams are not quite accurate. The inaccuracy really stems from motivation. Most of the writers of the articles indicate that because of poor previous customer relationships, these companies had no place to go but up. Additionally, the articles focused on the consolidation of power by a few key retailers to force manufacturers to have to change to survive and flourish. While I agree that many companies have significant customer relations problems, the change ultimately came about because suppliers *wanted* to work together with the customer instead of feeling like they *had* to!

In many ways, a subtle *Perestroika* has been going on within some key supplier-customer relationships. This change is taking place because the attitudes of forward-thinking suppliers are prevailing.

As a salesperson, I did not want to continually battle with my customers. I did not believe that significant progress was made if I beat my customers and won. This notion of winning usually means that somebody loses. I often thought, Why would anyone want to win at their customer's expense?

The last five years have seen significant turnover among the people who handle the majority of customer sales volume within most companies. This turnover, coupled with hiring good, new, open-minded people, has become infectious. Simultaneously, salespeople are now being trained in win-win relationships and are also being conditioned to accept long-term success (sometimes) at the expense of short-term results. This new pro-customer attitude is real and is becoming a way of life with the folks at some key suppliers in all industries. This way of life has manifested itself by involvement with key retailers via joint programs.

When you line up with key retailers in a specific marketing area, you are venturing towards ultimate regional marketing. The customer alignment process, while touted by the press as multifaceted, from information systems, to finance, to order processing, to delivery, to marketing, to joint venturism, has been somewhat overstated and has led some customers to believe that if they haven't been "teamed with," they have been unfairly treated.

What I've seen is really the opposite. Most companies' intention in aligning with *all* their customers is really to flush the inefficiencies out of mutual systems. Teaming does not always improve overall sales and marketing results. Clearly, volume and profit improvement are desirous, but this should be a product of the teaming process. Instead, I hear that people are glad about improving inventory and order-replenishment programs, resulting in customers having to carry less product inventory (which saves them money) and supplier deliveries arriving in a more timely fashion. This type of systems work should translate to all customers and then probably translate to customers working with their other suppliers, which are, in some cases, the competition.

Another common denominator in becoming closer to the customer is that sales and marketing organizations have had authority pushed downward. I have often encountered this result, both during my research for this book and from my own experience. The environment at the point-of-sale (over the desk, not in the store) is becoming revolutionary regarding how much flexibility a salesperson has with a customer. Because of this change, field people can design and work with customers on local/regional programs that formerly they had to pass on.

A final note on teaming: The death of teams is too many teams. Team only where there is significant upside potential—*do not over-team*.

A Duncan Hines Metamorphosis

To dramatize the change that has taken place, we need only look at two Duncan Hines examples. The first example happened several years ago when Duncan Hines introduced quick breads. The second example happened just recently with the introduction of Duncan Hines microwavable baking mixes.

The quick bread example is almost a classic case of how not to introduce a new item. It significantly dramatizes how far Procter & Gamble has come in understanding the customer. Remember that understanding the customer (channel of distribution) is fundamentally different from only understanding the consumer.

When Procter & Gamble first came out with Duncan Hines quick breads, the marketing group had not spoken thoroughly with the sales department nor any key customers regarding the most appropriate way to introduce this new product to the market. Instead, the brand relied upon the understanding that we had a competitive or slightly better product than the primary competition, Pillsbury. Duncan Hines was a good name to launch flanker products from, and we had significantly stronger advertising weights.

When the autopsy on this brand was done (the product did not survive more than two years), many factors were discussed. Continual cries were heard that the company doesn't do well introducing copied products. This was more an excuse than a reason. Frankly, the reason the quick bread introduction failed was a generally inferior introductory marketing program that did not attract appropriate trial levels. The marketing plan was flawed because the marketers did not consult their two customers: the sales force (internal) and the channel of distribution/grocery store (external). They blatantly disregarded the regional nature of the quick bread sub-category. They chose national marketing tactics that did not recognize regional differences and thus failed abysmally.

After the sales force had achieved superior national introductory distribution results, the first merchandising event was chosen to be a $1.19 prepriced promotion. This is a promotion that has $1.19 highlighted on the package to insinuate significant value to the consumer. This promotional device also offers a usually higher-than-normal margin to the customer. Introduction occurred shortly before the peak consumption period for quick breads so that the product could be established on the shelf and then merchandised off the shelf during peak consumption with this preprice. Everything seemed to be going well except that in a significant portion of the United States, competition was priced at 89 cents to 99 cents per package during peak consumption. Pillsbury did this by offering about an 80 cent per unit cost to the customer. Duncan Hines actually had a lower cost, mid-70 cents but stickered at $1.19. Duncan Hines introduced against a competitor that was well established and had a 20 cents per package retail price advantage to the consumer.

Since a brand's life can almost always be charted by how well it does during the first four to five months of launch, this marketing mistake during the critical introductory phase severely damaged the ability to succeed and ultimately led to discontinuation of the product.

Again, the postmortem shows many other conditions, but in my view everything was done right except talking to the sales force and the customers. If these audiences had been consulted, the marketing group would have known that an uncompetitive situation existed at the point of sale during this fragile introductory period.

Now let's take a look at a more recent Duncan Hines microwave mix introduction. The circumstances and conditions between microwave and quick bread, while not identical, are similar. Duncan Hines faced Pillsbury and Betty Crocker in the microwave baking mix category. Duncan Hines introduced their product prior to peak-consumption period after conducting a limited test market. The product was somewhat better tasting than the competition's and had a solid selling concept. The biggest difference, however, was that before the marketing plan was developed, the marketing group made a sincere effort to have the sales force input to the plan and regionalize it as best as they could. In addition, the brand and sales group went on several customer interviews to let our customers know what was about to be introduced, and shared specific marketing plans with them. The customers were then asked for their candid opinion. This external customer-interviewing technique was not new to the industry. I used it before I worked with Procter & Gamble, and other companies have been doing it for years. In fact, one vice president of merchandising I know is on the board of advisors for a major manufacturing company. The board of advisors keeps the company informed of industry changes and critiques new item plans.

Two examples have been reviewed within the same business category. One example failed mainly because marketing decision makers did not consult the sales force and the retailer (both customers). The second example took that extra step to understand the customers and their regional needs and was successful.

FINDING THE CUSTOMER—NEW CHANNELS

One of a regional marketer's most important directions should be to understand the "selling universe." Specifically, once the geographic boundaries have been established, the regional marketer should become a turf expert. Understanding the turf (geographic/demographic/regional characteristics) is only part of the understanding. Regional marketers should completely understand the channels of distribution that currently exist, as well as explore the options of new channels. Some companies are good at this, and some are not. Many companies have become complacent relative to expanding their mature business into new channel opportunities. This usually is a function of upper management's view on new business expansion and whether or not the "intrapreneurial" spirit is rewarded and recognized. Needless to say, it is important for the regional marketing (and management) system to assess current business and identify new business. Once this is done, you can engage in the next logical function of understanding the customer.

HOW TO UNDERSTAND THE CUSTOMER

While my interviews, research, and practical experience led me to a list of several "how-to's," there are basically four key focus areas:

1. Do Your Homework
Strive to understand as much as possible about the customer at large to whom you want to sell and market, and, if possible, the individual who represents the company. Take this very seriously.

Learning about a customer should surely be a prerequisite if you have never called on the customer, but should be an ongoing responsibility of people who have established accounts. When doing homework on the customer, make sure the objectives of the individual representing the company are carefully understood. Oftentimes the individual company representative you deal with may not have aligned objectives with the company at large. This incongruity exists often and at most levels of organizations. When faced with this conflict, focus on serving the long-term or primary customer. The company you are selling to is the host of the company representative—it is the primary customer. It is important to recognize the conditions of your secondary customer, the representative, as you ultimately try to service the primary. It is also critical to understand how the company representative is recognized and rewarded.

Remember, the concept of customer homework is an ongoing one and essential for continual improvement in servicing the account. During a recent interview, I was asked, "What would you say is the most significant responsibility a salesperson and marketer should have?" I unhesitatingly responded that a salesperson at any level should be a *sincere student* of the customer, then a leader who advocates *mutually* beneficial business plans. A marketer, on the other hand, should *first* own a truly superior understanding of the consumer, and *secondly* a strong awareness of the customer.

2. *Interview the Customer*
Try to understand the customer's wants and needs and how they measure success.

I recently spoke to a group of radio promotion and sales managers. In this case, I was their customer. When asked to give the number one reason for their failing to make the sale, I reinforced the theme that they generally failed to interview their customer. As Karl Ball, senior marketing director for Local Marketing Corporation says, "Sellers often approach me with packaged solutions (their programs) in search of opportunities—instead, they should ask me to describe opportunities that I, in fact, have, so that they could develop appropriate solutions."

I also am very familiar with The Precept Group, an advisory firm specializing in corporate benefits and compensation programs, located in Newport Beach, California, and spoke at length with one of the cofounders, Alex Wasilewski. He had been a regional marketing vice president for a much larger national company and had been very successful. His success obviously is carrying over to his somewhat smaller regional venture. I asked him what he would identify as a key to success. He indicated that the most succinct answer is provided by their clients:

Our clients tell us that our firm's sole intention and focus is on researching their needs and wants. Our firm then tries to satisfy their wants with integrity, quality thought process, hard work, an effective process to deliver on our promises, and, finally, a method of managing results.

From the customer's perspective, it is clear why The Precept Group is successful.

3. Identify, Clearly Understand, Then Deliver on Behalf of the Customer's Expectations

There is a saying that goes, "Underpromise and overdeliver." While ideally I would like to promise something, develop an expectation, and then exactly deliver that promise, if I had to err, I would rather err on the underpromise side. Generally, customers do have an attitude of *what have you done for me lately?* Hopefully, over time, you will develop, as will your products, enough equity with a customer that when the exception happens (hopefully, it *is* the exception) and you don't quite meet your customer's expectation, they will spend some of your equity against you and allow you some leeway.

About a year ago, some Procter & Gamble managers conducted an interview with a key customer. As a result of that interview, the four Procter & Gamble managers clearly heard (or thought they heard) the customer's two key vice presidents express an interest in talking to somebody about regional marketing. I was selected for the follow-up meeting with these two vice presidents and knew within 30 seconds that our expectations were not aligned. I began discussing the principles and fundamentals of regional marketing and how they could relate to the account. However, they did not hide their dismay as they awaited an expected specific proposal about a joint regional marketing venture. Needless to say, I felt like the gentleman on the Federal Express commercial who gets up before the sales meeting without his slides and does finger artwork on a blank screen.

After we left, one of the managers bemoaned the fact that this particular account had not sent any signals that their expectation was a specific proposal. Frankly, while I believed him, I also shared the quote, "What is is, is not what is is, what is is, is what your customer perceives is is." This speaks specifically to customer's perceptions, which are closely linked to expectations. If you understand customers' perceptions about the way they see their business being conducted, then you will get a strong clue as to their expectations.

4. The "Ostrich Syndrome" or Asking for Feedback

In his book *How to Win Customers and Keep Them for Life*, Michael LeBoeuf, Ph.D., talks about the Ostrich Syndrome. In his discussion of the Ostrich Syndrome, he quotes Dr. Robert Anthony: "If you stick your head in the sand, one thing is for sure, you'll get your rear kicked." Dr. LeBoeuf contends that you should develop a regular routine of asking customers, "How are we doing?" and "How can we get better?"[1]

It is essential to maintain faith to this principle or assume that strong customer understanding will erode over time. Don't allow the Ostrich Syndrome to exist; routinely check in with how your customers think you are doing. An important twist is to have local managers ask their local accounts for feedback. Since there is significant chance for misunderstanding, make sure you have the feedback solicited by people who can understand it. Regional marketing starts with regional understanding.

SUMMARY

Understanding your customer is the most important variable in the marketing assessment process for *sales* people to master. If the salesperson has at least an *average* product or service (priced fairly) and a *reasonable* understanding of the other three variables (the consumer, their own company, and the competition),

---

[1] Michael LeBoeuf, Ph.D., "To Keep Customers for Life, Ask the Platinum Questions," *How to Win Customers and Keep Them for Life* (New York: The Berkley Publishing Group, 1987), p. 66.

the seller will almost always be successful if they have an exceptional understanding of the customer.

While it is important to a company, regardless of regional implication, to understand the customer, it is critical if you are executing any kind of regional strategy. Key customers on a national basis can have their impact diluted significantly. It is not uncommon for a sales region to have a very large customer that could make up 25 percent of the region's business. This customer is critical to the region's business, whereas nationally this customer might represent less than one percent of the overall sales. This variance of impact needs to be recognized and arbitrated. A company with a regional marketing attitude will always recognize the customer's value to a region instead of explaining it away as a small piece of the national pie.

SUMMARY CHECKLIST

1. *Have you researched your turf to identify new business opportunities?*

2. *Have you done your homework on your customer's company at large? Have you done your homework on the person you will directly deal with who represents the customer?*

3. *Do you know how the customer's representative is measured? Do you know how the company measures itself? Do you know the difference between their wants and needs?*

4. *Have you clearly identified and understood your customer's expectations?*

5. *Have you incorporated the request for feedback into your operation? Do you have enough courage to ask for ways to improve your operation?*

Chapter Ten

Understanding Your Consumer

INTRODUCTION

The advertising/marketing organization should have an intimate understanding of the consumer. As previously mentioned, the sales function should become an expert on the customer. The regional marketer, however, should become a master of both. Since, historically, most marketing has been focused on the consumer, you would think that the advertisers have it easy and the sellers are doing all the leg work understanding this new customer focus. Reality couldn't be further from the truth. While the customer is becoming more important and attracting more and more of the available marketing dollars, the customer base is shrinking. Retailers and dealers seem to be consolidating and acting more alike than ever before.

NATIONAL VERSUS REGIONAL CONSUMER

Understanding the consumer is critical to regional marketing and is, in many ways, a distinguishing point between national mass marketing and true regional marketing. National mass marketers select a standardized approach that frankly, for years has been very effective and in many situations is still the best approach. National marketing treats the consumer as one homogeneous entity. This approach is simpler and usually more cost-effective. This style does not purposefully attempt to insult or ignore various groups (ethnic or regional) or consumers, but this tactic seems to get the best results.

As competition for this increasingly more aware and selective consumer heats up, smart companies are becoming much more regional and targeted in their approaches. They still run national programs (advertising and promotion) focused on their perception of the mainstream consumer, but they are also adjusting their efforts whenever they come in contact with a large ethnic or regional group of consumers. This adjustment, which to some companies is now an investment, will reap dividends in the future.

Understanding consumers' wants and motivations on a regional basis is very sound business. As different regions refine their own distinct personalities, marketers will do well to stay on top of the changes. This is vital because of what seems to be a subtle shifting of influence from the supplier to the retailer. As the customer or trade channel gets more power and starts to dominate this seller-customer relationship, manufacturers can employ only two key strategies. One is the teaming approach. The other is a direct manufacturer-to-consumer bonding approach. This bonding should be taken seriously, because it is a way to preserve brand loyalty. To preserve what is left of this relationship or to build it anew takes a true understanding of the consumer. Just to understand the consumer in a broad sense (national) is not good enough. The 1990s and beyond will demand a specific understanding of the *various* regional consumers. This level of understanding is analogous to an undergraduate degree versus an advanced degree. Needless to say, I believe we need more consumer Ph.D.'s!

Green Marketing

Green marketing is a term that is generally used to describe marketing that strongly considers the environment. Much has been written and reported regarding environmental actions and legislation as they relate to all kinds of products. This started several years ago with the move toward unleaded gasoline. Today, it is taking shape in areas like plastics. If there was ever an opportunity for companies to help their business, help their corporate image, and help the world at large, it is in the area of green marketing. Additionally, this is an area that must be monitored and managed on a regional basis. A quick review of state-by-state solid waste legislation would show some states (at this writing) with no regulatory or legislative activity pending. Reciprocally, you would find states like Maine that, as far back as 1989, passed a bill that banned aseptic containers and six-pack rings. Additionally, in Maine, retailers are required to use paper bags instead of plastic bags. I strongly believe that the issue of green marketing could make or break companies in the future. Companies must be in tune with local state legislation, as it generally reflects the will of the individual consumer. This legislation will *absolutely* accelerate and become more environmental friendly. This potential will become reality and will affect all disciplines that a company engages in, from research and development, to product supply, to advertising, to finance, to marketing and sales. Companies should not wait until specific regional legislation spreads and becomes national. By then, it will be too late, and proactive companies will already have revised products, packaging, and programs to leverage this feature into a strong customer and consumer benefit. Green marketing is not the next Nehru shirt. Paying attention to the environment within all industries is here to stay and will take on expanded consumer, customer, and supplier importance.

When I speak about environmentally friendly or unfriendly products and programming, I also conceptually expand this to healthy versus nonhealthy foods. Certainly, I would want to be a company that regionally understands this growing consumer movement relative to healthy foods and environmentally friendly products.

Regional Product Differentiation

Because of the issues of health and green marketing, regional product differentiation does come into play. Beyond these reasons, it is also wise for businesses to recognize regional product opportunities. These opportunities may be different relative to size, style, and/or economic considerations. Several companies engage in regional product differentiation strategies, and most of these directions are fundamentally targeted to satisfy regional consumer and customer differences. Another reason is to achieve more tactical business flexibility. Regardless of the motivations, it is necessary to make sure the difference can be leveraged, based upon the regional consumer and the customer.

CONSUMER HUNTING

To find the consumer, you must know for whom you are looking. There is a saying, "Any road will get you there if you don't know where you are going." Such is the case when your brand or product group does not have regional strategies congruent with a national strategy.

Assuming you have set strategies for your product that take into account regional differences and ethnic concentrations, you are chartered to go "consumer hunting." Subject to the target consumer profile you have for your product, you can access volumes of information. The government (both federal and state) profiles its citizens by all sorts of demographic characteristics. Additionally, marketing services have sophisticated models that target consumers based upon race, income, family size, and other variables. Then, they sort these by zip code so that you can actually call or direct-mail consumers with a reasonable degree of accuracy. Generally, radio, television, and even billboard companies also have this information and have developed programs to help marketers.

When I was interested in a program targeted to Hispanics in the Miami market, I had little more to do than call up Ackerly Communications Company. This group already had billboard locations near customer grocery stores and had Hispanic neighborhoods already charted. They even had a targeted program already developed (a specific number of billboards at key locations) and ready for purchase.

CONSUMERS' WAYS AND MEANS

While consumers do tend to relocate frequently, their basic patterns of community choice generally remain constant. Also, if changes in patterns do occur, they usually change gradually over time, and these variations can be recognized and planned for.

Such is not the case, however, when suddenly various areas of the country plunge into a recession or blast into a runaway positive economic cycle. These regional changes happen quickly (a year or so) and usually happen one region at a time. How often have we seen this occur in the real estate industry? When external factors arise (such as economic), your consumers' ways and means are severely affected. Regional marketers should serve an early warning function. To intimately understand the impact of external variables on consumers, marketers should conduct focus groups, which if conducted well, provide valuable intelligence that can sculpt the way we market.

Having a regional marketing attitude, even if you don't have a program, is critical in times of transition. Regional marketers are on the front end of change because they are part of it. Since they are physically located in the region, they read the papers. Actually, they are the very regional consumers that they market to. This is in contrast to marketers who are located in headquarters and are somewhat insulated by having broader responsibility and by physical proximity. Of course, the national marketers will say they rely on their regional salespeople for interpretation of business conditions; but local salespeople are usually too "macho" to blame general economic conditions for a slowdown in sales. They generally believe they can succeed, given the right price and marketing program. Rarely does sales proclaim that business has slowed down as a result of a sluggish regional economy. Therefore, there should be an existing marketing presence in key business regions.

Mazda Motors of America—the Regional Touch

"Because Mazda Motors of America values regional marketing, they were prepared for the oil bust that occurred in the Gulf States Region in 1986 through 87," said Randy Pressgrove, Dealer Development Manager.

> Well, I guess I should rephrase that and say we saw it coming and took proactive measures to lessen the impact. We saw a gradual decrease in oil-drilling activity. That decline accelerated. While a lot of people in an absolute sense didn't lose their jobs, this slowdown was picked up by the media and really started affecting the general regional population's desire to make major personal purchases. You will remember this was about the same time that various other parts of the country, such as the Northeast and the West Coast, were in the middle of very strong economic growth. If Mazda had taken a totally national approach to marketing and sales, we would have been in a very tough position. We had just introduced a new generation RX-7 sports car, and we were about to introduce our new luxury 929 to the U.S. market. Nationally, the focus was on a more expensive luxury car. We in the Gulf Region went quickly off from that strategy and immediately reduced our luxury inventory. We loaded up with less-expensive utilitarian models and base pickup trucks. My low-end sales skyrocketed, and I was able to hold my overall volume. When the "oil patch" began to pull out of the regional recession, the Gulf was much better prepared to enjoy the improving regional economy.

Mr. Pressgrove reaffirmed that because the company had an attitude toward regional marketing and trained people in place, they were on the front end of this change and could act in a much more proactive way.

ETHNIC MARKETING

In a discussion of regional marketing, ethnic marketing must receive extensive treatment. I will not address all the different ethnic groups in this section. Instead, I will use data for Hispanics and Asians to illustrate my points.

A couple of companies I spoke with categorized their regional effort as totally ethnic-driven. This was similar to some companies who summarized their regional effort as totally special events driven. This very focused approach to regional marketing can work, but it is not full-service regional marketing. Ethnic, like special events, is but a singular style.

Companies are wise to tread slowly when integrating the ethnic variable into either their regional or national efforts. In fact, many mistakes have been made by companies who chose to treat ethnic marketing as a national program. Once again, the regional variable should not be subordinated to an ethnic focus. Said another way, ethnic marketing should not be considered vertical marketing.

VERTICAL MARKETING (BEWARE)

As the robot of the 1960s, television series *Lost in Space* was known to say, "Danger! Danger! Danger!" When attempting to vertically sell or market to a particular customer or consumer group, *be careful*. Vertical marketing occurs when you make a decision that, because groups of customers or consumers are alike, you can sell or market to them the same way. This can work when you are selling to 100 individual stores of the same chain. This may be a preferred style, especially if the chain has an effective centrally managed operation. This vertical approach targeted to all Hispanic consumers, on the other hand, can be very embarrassing and costly. Hispanics are spread out regionally across the United States. The type of Hispanic marketing program you should use is subject to which region you are in. This is a function of ethnic origin. Hispanics from the southwestern United States are primarily of Mexican origin. Hispanics from the southeastern United States, principally Florida, are generally of Cuban descent. Hispanics in the northeastern United States, principally the New York City area, are typically of Puerto Rican heritage. To treat these three regions and their Hispanic consumers as one does not recognize the cultural differences inherent in their different primary origins. As if this isn't cause enough for concern, these three origins dominate the Hispanic residents of the United States, but the category of "other," meaning residents who have origin from a country other than Mexico, Cuba, and Puerto Rico, is huge. In fact, the "other" category is larger than either Cuban or Puerto Rican.

Following are a few examples of marketing efforts by companies who did not recognize the importance of origin difference. I firmly believe that if regional marketers had existed within these markets, they would have prevented these marketing misses.

Braniff Airlines

Braniff made a classic Blooper, when the airline's ads told Hispanics to fly *en cuero* . . . or naked.[1]

Tropicana

Tropicana advertised *jugo de china* in Miami. *China* means orange to Puerto Ricans, but Miami's Cubans thought it was juice from the Orient.[2]

---

[1] Sarah Smith, "If You Want a Big, New Market . . . ," *Fortune* (November 21, 1988), p. 181.

[2] Ibid.

Jack-in-the-Box

Jack-in-the-Box goofed with a commercial featuring a band of Mexican mariachis accompanying a Spanish flamenco dancer. "That's like having Willie Nelson sing while Michael Jackson does the moonwalk," says Bert Valencia, a marketing professor at the American Graduate School of International Management in Glendale, Arizona.[3]

U.S. Army

The U.S. Army tried to figure out why its English language campaign was missing many of the young Hispanics it was designed to reach. The Army discovered that Hispanic recruits aged 18 to 24 watched English-language TV, but their parents relied on Spanish media. "We found that 61.9 percent of Hispanics said they go first to their parents for advice," says Major Gregory McGuckin, chief of media and distribution, "so we began advertising to them in Spanish." The Army says Hispanic enlistments are up.[4]

The Blushing Executives

Testing ad campaigns is important, yet often ignored. A little pretesting might have saved some companies embarrassment. Even if Hispanics design a campaign, it's no guarantee that they are familiar with all Hispanic groups. The word *bichos*, for example, means bugs to Mexicans; to Puerto Ricans it means a man's private parts. An insecticide company's posters guaranteeing to kill all *bichos* left executives blushing.[5]

---

[3] Ibid.

[4] Ibid, p. 184.

[5] Ibid, pp. 187–188.

This Author's Near Miss

A particular brand group came to me with test radio copy that would target Hispanic consumers in both the Miami and Los Angeles markets. I was quick enough to recognize that Miami Hispanics and Los Angeles Hispanics react differently to the particular product because of their different cultural backgrounds. Score one for me. However, the text of the radio copy identified the women as head of the household. I didn't have a problem with that, because traditionally women influence the majority of grocery-purchase decisions. When I shared a copy of the text with my Miami-based salespeople (many of whom were of Hispanic origin), they bristled. They (both the men and women) felt that this statement could be slightly offensive because, to Hispanics, the man is the classical head of the household. The commercial never ran.

The Emergence of Promotion

It is important to understand and learn from the mistakes of others. It is equally important to understand and identify trends. One current trend is the growing importance of promotion and special events as they relate to Hispanic marketing. As would be expected from national mass marketers, advertising was the marketing first-choice and still dominates the marketing dollar allocation. However, as you can see from Figure 10–1, a transition is underway. Both advertising and local promotional spending is increasing in the absolute. However, promotion expenditure is increasing at a much higher rate. This is predictable because marketers are always testing the mix of their dollars. A real story will be told if in coming years the absolute dollar amount invested in advertising actually levels off and drops while promotion spending continues to increase.

Figure 10–1
More Motion in Promotions

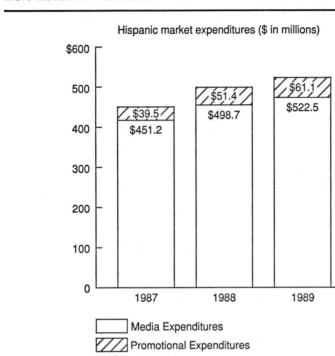

Hispanic market expenditures ($ in millions)

Media Expenditures
Promotional Expenditures

Source: Christy Fisher, "Promotions Trickle Turns into Torrent," *Advertising Age* (October 15, 1990), p. 42.

ENVIRONMENT VERSUS HEREDITY

In the seventh grade, I was part of a panel debate in my health and science class on the issue of which variable shapes a person's life more: the environment or heredity. Little did I know that several years later I would wrestle with that very issue regarding ethnic and regional marketing. Which of these variables should prevail when it comes to regional marketing or any type of marketing? My conclusion is that while both have to be considered, I would most often look toward the regional element to begin my planning. Since the United States is such a melting pot of diverse cultures and economic scenarios, we must possess a superior understanding of the region or turf. We should not only understand the different ethnic and socioeconomic profiles, but we should also understand the climate, the public events, and important trends as they relate to all issues. We should also account for and understand any important aberrations. For example, you can bet that local bottlers and regionally oriented national companies took quick notice when 12,000 Hmong refugees from Laos settled in St. Paul.[6] On a larger scale, but beneath most large national companies' marketing radars, are the approximately 200,000 people of Middle Eastern descent in Detroit. Impressively, some 1,500 small grocery and convenience stores in this vicinity are owned by a whole subculture of Chaldean Christians with roots in Iraq.[7]

"So What! What Does This All Mean to Me?"

That quote was uttered to me as a friend was aggressively reviewing this chapter of the book. What this means to companies is critical. Much is happening with the consumer in America. In this chapter, I have only begun to open up the topic of understanding the consumer. If you believe the population statisticians, the future will see much more ethnic, financial, and family-size change. Also, population is constantly redistributing. The majority of companies are paying only tacit attention to this change because they don't own regional understandings. Instead, they chase total domestic, and, in some cases, global, understandings. The gradual regional changes are too difficult to see because there is too much information to be digested on national and global

---

[6] William A. Henry III, "Beyond the Melting Pot," *Time* (April 9, 1990), p. 29.
[7] Ibid.

levels. For example, it shouldn't have come as a surprise to my Puritan oil brand contact that over 20 percent of the households in the New York City area are Jewish. Additionally, we have more than twice our national brand share on Puritan cooking oil in Jewish households in New York City. People in the brand seemed surprised by this until they found out that Jewish people generally are very health-conscious and that three years earlier we ran a kosher Puritan oil promotion targeting New York City. These brand marketers are not dumb and uncaring; they are just preoccupied with the big-picture level of the business they manage. The downside is that while they look at the top line, the bottom line can be changing region by region.

Regional marketing brings the antenna and radar into the marketing trenches. The changes with the consumer and customer are not generally happening in most companies' headquarters cities. As Filiberto Fernandez, manager of Hispanic markets for Polaroid said, "You can't stay holed up on the 30th floor and expect to understand how Hispanics think." Fernandez takes them (key executives) on junkets to Miami, 1,200 miles south and light-years away from the company's Cambridge, Massachusetts, headquarters. "I give them Hispanic Marketing 101."[8]

It seems as though most companies wait until changes among consumers expand from regional to national before they lock on to consumer patterns. Often, by this time they have missed the opportunity to market at the grassroots level in the early stages of either ethnic development or consumer phenomenon. Some companies, however, especially in retailing, are quick to see regional consumer opportunities and jump on them. They recognize that a regional fad or trend can explode across the country and can be high-dollar volume and short-lived. An example of this is The May Company.

---

[8] Smith, "If You Want a Big, New Market . . . ," p. 182.

The May Company

The May Company is comprised of several leading department stores from around the country, like Lord and Taylor, Filene's, Foleys, Robinsons, Famous Barr, and others. Richard Bennet, senior vice president for Famous Barr, believes in the collection of strong regional retailers coming together under the banner of one strong company. He also indicates that they have a not-so-secret weapon, teleconferencing, that helps them all stay on top of regional and national trends.

> Monday morning teleconferencing hooks all the senior merchandising managers together to discuss trends. We discuss what's hot and what's not and then try to understand if what is working in Boston is particular to the region, or could it have broader application to business in St. Louis. These conferences have proven to become vital to our business, as we could quickly tell that Batman merchandise was going to be great business everywhere while Dick Tracy merchandise was not going to make it. This gives us the ability to quickly adjust our inventories.

Mr. Bennet is also quick to add:

> We are empowered locally to make regional decisions, which gives us the flexibility that national chains don't seem to have. For example: I carry a brand of shoe called Etienne-Aigner which sells very well in St. Louis. For whatever reasons, my competition doesn't stock the product. Because I have control over my local product mix, I am at a significant advantage.

Mr. Bennet summarized his situation with a concern:

> Regional marketing and local decision making is [sic] giving us a strong advantage in today's business framework. We seem to be able to outmaneuver big national competitors very easily. If our competition ever decides to empower its people and allow them to make the same kinds of decisions that I make, then this business will get much more difficult. Competition already has built in national purchasing efficiencies; if they ever let their people really market regionally, it could level the playing field. The key here is understanding the regional consumer as well as the competition in each market. I really believe that both my competition and I actually have a similar understanding of the consumer; it's

just that I can do something regionally with that understanding, while my competition gets bogged down in national considerations which may not be right for the local situation.

Other companies are also wise to the ever-changing consumer, both on ethnic levels and in a much broader sense.

Metropolitan Life Insurance Company

Metropolitan Life Insurance Company is developing a strong reputation as a sharp regional marketer. One of the keys to this effort is a focus against ethnic marketing. Metropolitan Life has successfully targeted both the Chinese and Korean communities through foreign language ads and by increasing its Asian-American sales staff.

Metropolitan Life also increased sales of insurance to Hispanics over 150 percent in 1988 with Spanish ads targeted at strongly Hispanic regions. The company chose to use Latin actors rather than Snoopy, the cartoon mainstay of its English ads, but not a big attraction for Hispanics.[9]

Campbell's

Campbell's is one of the preeminent consumer packaged-goods regional marketers. In fact, Campbell's was one of the first large manufacturers to restructure its sales and marketing organizations to become more regionalized. It is very apparent today in almost all that Campbell's does that they value both customer and consumer relationships. Campbell's is always putting "top spin" on national promotions to relate more with the local consumer. In addition to adjusting national programs, Campbell's develops grassroots promotions to appeal directly to consumers, whether it be ethnic-driven, local sports-related, or just community relations-motivated.

---

[9] Ibid, p. 181.

FIGURE 10–2
Growth in Population, by Region 1980–2000

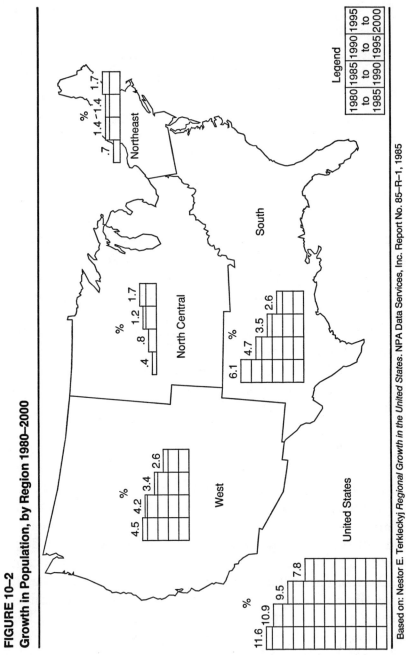

Based on: Nestor E. Terkleckyj *Regional Growth in the United States.* NPA Data Services, Inc. Report No. 85–R–1, 1985

Source: Dr. William Lazer et al., "The Demographic Vision," *Marketing 2000 and Beyond,* American Marketing Association, p. 73.

THE CHANGING CONSUMER

The emergence of various ethnic groups, the graying of America, the significant migration of people to states like Arizona, New Mexico, and Florida, and the prediction that by approximately 2050 to 2075 whites could be a minority in this country are marketing dynamite. Once you get beyond the shock of this future-state reality, you can't help but get excited as a marketer or seller working in this environment.

To understand just what kinds of changes and shifts are occurring, let's review the following charts and their applications to regional marketing.

Figure 10–2 identifies broad growth in population by region. The review period is from 1980 through the year 2000. Figures 10–3 and 10–4 show the five fastest percentage growth states and the five slowest percentage growth states during both 1980 through 1990 (for perspective) and 1990 through 2000 (for planning).

Application

This population migration data has been available for quite some time, and it's amazing how marketing and sales management at large generally ignore it. In fact, of the several marketing managers I questioned regarding population shift data, only one marketer even said they account for it when it comes time to do regional marketing budgets and regional sales projections. Not so surprising was the response from sales management types. While they would seem to be most affected over time by these shifts, they responded very passively about the consequences these numbers had on their sales objectives.

While I can relate to this general apathy about impact, I argue that each year both marketers and sellers ought to understand whether or not they have more or fewer consumers than the previous year. This should become increasingly more

FIGURE 10–3
Fastest Growing States

1980–1990		1990–2000	
Alaska	43%	Arizona	23%
Arizona	38%	Nevada	21%
Nevada	35%	New Mexico	21%
Florida	32%	Florida	20%
New Mexico	25%	Georgia	19%

Source: Adapted from *The Wall Street Journal*, November 17, 1988, p. B1.

FIGURE 10–4
Slowest Growing States

1980–1990		1990–2000	
Iowa	5.4%	Iowa	7.6%
W. Virginia	4.8%	W. Virginia	7.3%
Pennsylvania	0.3%	N. Dakota	4.7%
Ohio	0.1%	Pennsylvania	2.7%
Michigan	+0.3%	Wyoming	2.6%

Source: Adapted from *The Wall Street Journal*, November 17, 1988, p. B1.

relevant and important when you descend from a broad regional analysis to a by-state analysis to a by-city-within-state analysis. These reports exist and can reveal some wide growth swings within states. It is important to many people to understand the different growth rates of Orlando, Jacksonville Tampa, Miami, and Pensacola all within the high growth state of Florida. Unless I'm missing something, this information can be used to help forecast results and, more importantly, manage expectations.

On another level, it is very important to understand the overall growth rates of various ethnic groups. Figure 10–5 clearly shows the change in absolute population and percentage for Asian Americans. Interestingly, this chart stimulated a discussion that typifies the classical regional versus national marketing paradigm. When discussing this with a marketer, he was quick to point out that the projected approximately 10 million Asian Americans in the United States represented only about 4 percent of the total population. What he failed to

**FIGURE 10–5
The Changing Asian-
American Population
(projections for 1990 and
2000)**

1990		
Ethnic Group	Number	Percent
Filipino	1,405,146	21.5%
Chinese	1,259,038	19.3
Vietnamese	859,638	13.2
Korean	814,495	12.5
Japanese	804,535	12.3
Asian Indian	684,339	10.5
Other Asian	706,417	10.8

2000		
Ethnic Group	Number	Percent
Filipino	2,070,571	21.0%
Chinese	1,683,537	17.1
Vietnamese	1,574,385	16.0
Korean	1,320,759	13.4
Asian Indian	1,006,305	10.2
Japanese	856,619	8.7
Other Asian	1,338,188	13.6

Source: Leon F. Bouvier and Anthony Agresta, Population Reference Bureau, Washington, D.C.

Source: *The Wall Street Journal*, July 20, 1989, p. B1.

initially recognize is that the majority of these 10 million potential Asian American consumers reside on the West Coast and therefore make up a much larger percentage of that region's population. Furthermore, the majority of these consumers reside in a very small number of cities which make up an even greater percentage of the cities' populations. The same situation exists with most ethnic groups and, therefore, marketing to them regionally is not very difficult. With only reasonable effort and probably much less than this segment's fair share of the marketing budget (4 percent), the results for some product groups would most likely outperform the balance of all other markets on a percentage growth basis.

Black Ethnic Marketing

Before I leave this chapter on Understanding Your Consumer, it is important to discuss marketing to the largest ethnic group in the United States, black Americans. The ethnic group that really paved the way for minority-targeted marketing is not really considered hot anymore. The ethnic groups to target are Hispanics and Asian Americans. Of course, these other groups possess incredible growth rates through the 1980s:

Asian Americans	55%
Hispanics	34%
Blacks	12%
Whites	4%

Source: William A. Henry III, "Beyond the Melting Pot," *Time*, April 9, 1990.

It is also true that median family incomes are trending higher for all other groups than blacks. Regionally, many companies are missing great opportunities by not having focused programs towards black consumers. This is confusing, as there is more data on marketing to blacks than we have for all other ethnic groups combined. When focusing on these other groups, we should first test market to make sure we don't miss our objective. With black ethnic marketing, we have already jumped the learning curve. Beyond all this, we must face the fact that there are currently more black Americans than Hispanic Americans and Asian Americans combined. This represents strong spending power that warrants immediate attention. Some companies really understand this (McDonald's, Burger King, PepsiCo and Coca-Cola) and will reap dividends amongst the black consumers regionally and nationally.

Black Rodeo in New York City

You read that correctly. For two years, going on three, Procter & Gamble has been a primary sponsor of a Black Rodeo series in the Greater New York Boroughs. This program is the vision of a wonderful man, Dr. George Blair. I became involved with this program after it had been rejected by our special events group. The notion of a series of real rodeos with black cowboys and cowgirls in conjunction with our selling several of our products in local supermarkets seemed just wacky enough to make sense. I put together a group of five brands and sponsored the program. The program was easily a financial success, and it went a small step toward making a social difference.

My point here is this: there are many black rodeo type promotions (with a little imagination) as well as other classical marketing opportunities that would deliver results. Marketing to blacks is not like traveling through uncharted water. Blacks generally are brand loyal, and because blacks are spread out much more than most ethnic groups, there is the possibility to market more conventionally (yes, even more nationally) than to all the other groups.

SUMMARY

Somebody has to own an understanding of consumers and that somebody *should* be the marketing organization. Really understanding both consumer differences and similarities can translate to very efficient on-target marketing. The best level at which to understand consumers is regionally. It is not now, or never has been, correct to consider any ethnic group (whites included) as identically similar. Too many companies have made too many mistakes in marketing to consumers by using a cookie cutter approach. Understanding consumers regionally manages the risk of mistakes and allows you to customize your efforts in a more practical way.

Smart companies treat consumers personally by treating them regionally. These companies develop their consumer expertise by making a significant investment in information and technology to become one with the consumer. The more that companies know about their target consumers, the more successful those companies will be. Customers/Trade Channels are becoming more and more knowledgeable about their consumers. Manufacturers and distributors do not have the leisure to sit back and allow their customers to become exponentially smarter. A well-qualified understanding of consumers is becoming a prerequisite for customer-supplier credibility.

SUMMARY CHECKLIST

1. *What is your regional product strategy?*
2. *Who is your regional target consumer?*
3. *How do you find that consumer?*
4. *If that consumer is from an emerging new ethnic group, what cultural and procedural "watch outs" should be recognized?*
5. *What is the best way to sell to that ethnic consumer? Is the consumer easier to advertise to? Does the consumer react well to special events or promotions? Is the particular consumer price-sensitive? Does product or service quality have more of a priority?*
6. *Should you introduce a product variation (say, more spices in a particular sauce or soup), or should you introduce your existing product?*
7. *What are the regional characteristics of the turf that your consumer lives in? Is the area in an upswing economically? Is the area fairly stable or declining?*
8. *Should you delegate the marketing and advertising (and possibly selling) function to a regional independent broker or advertising/marketing agency?*
9. *Is there long-term opportunity with this consumer? Specifically, if you make an investment, will you eventually get a return on that investment?*

Ultimate Regional Marketing

I n Section I, we positioned regional marketing at large and its growing importance in domestic and international business. We also recognized two special factors in understanding regional marketing: (1) special events as a mainstay style, and (2) the special circumstances that occur when you bring marketing and sales together in one functional focus.

In Section II, we learned about the general principles that need to exist (systems/conditions, selection, training, and empowerment) to give regional marketing a chance to work. We further reviewed some very specific principles and guidelines as they relate to the individual marketing mix elements of promotion, pricing, and advertising.

Section III paid special attention to an approach called the Marketing Assessment Process (MAP), which has universal application not only to regional marketing but to national marketing. This approach demands an understanding of the competition, customer, consumer, yourself, and your turf.

The three previous sections of this book set the stage for Section IV. This section has two chapters. The first is "Regional Brand Strategies." This chapter focuses on a strategic style with which I have a lot of personal experience. To me, the development of regional brand strategies is the only correct way to execute regional marketing.

The second chapter is called Customer-ized Marketing. This is a specific direction that goes beyond general trade marketing and calls for a thorough understanding of the customers within a particular region. This style of marketing is leading-edge, has some risk, but can produce huge rewards. Customer-ized marketing can be a sub-set of regional brand strategies or can stand alone.

I can't stress enough the importance of these two chapters. These are the last two chapters of the book and they are the "product" of the book. The previous three sections are the process and contain special situations. For lack of a better expression, Sections 1 through 3 are the prerequisites for ultimate regional marketing.

Chapter Eleven

Regional Brand Strategies

INTRODUCTION

One of the executions to use to implement regional marketing is regional brand strategies. The careful development and deployment of regional brand strategies is essential for regional marketing to continue as a justifiable strategy. Without the development of key regional brand strategies, your business plans are nothing more than tactics looking for a purpose.

The development and faithfulness of this regional focus takes a reasonable amount of time and work, but, from personal experience, I submit that it is worthwhile.

CORPORATE LANGUAGE

To begin our work with regional brand strategies, we need to start with a series of working definitions. These definitions may differ slightly from the dictionary, but the key thing to remember is that these are *working* definitions. The need for a common language is critical for understanding and efficiency. It is as important in the corporation for the different functional disciplines (sales, marketing, manufacturing, finance, and research and development) as it is for the different branches of the military. In my experience dealing with companies, I have noticed that continuity of definitions is sorely lacking. This is not only a problem between the functional disciplines of companies but within the specific functions themselves. It is not surprising for me to find some people's strategies becoming other people's tactics. Also, the terms *goal* and *objective* are almost universally confused.

Please accept the following as working definitions to aid in understanding this chapter and, thus, regional brand strategies. In addition, the following terms are actually the sequential steps in the regional brand strategy model, shown in Figure 11–2 later in this chapter.

GLOSSARY

Vision (Step 1)

Vision is a mental picture of what you consider to be future state. There is a saying that bad breath is better than no breath at all. This holds true in the area of vision. Visions are purposefully abstract and vague. A vision is an image of how you want your company, brand, service, or general end-state to be. In many ways, it is the "light at the end of the tunnel." You can't quite discern the light, but it is the direction you want to follow. When I have worked with groups in the past, I've had them sketch their "fantasy island" to help begin the visioning process, whether it be personal or corporate.

Mission (Step 2)

Mission is a profound statement of purpose or a general reason for being. The mission should be simple, easy to understand, and directionally positive and valid. The mission, in many ways, is what we do for a living. It should help move you to your vision.

Values (Step 3)

I firmly believe that every organization should have a value statement. Values such as honesty, straight talk, belief in personal responsibility, and ownership serve as good periodic checks and balances to guide your business plan. If one of your corporate values is to be fair to your customers, then anything you strategically or tactically do that is not fair should be thrown out of your plan. If you defy your value statements, then you ultimately lie to yourself, a situation that should alter your reason for being and/or your mission.

> *Author's Note: It will be assumed and generally not discussed throughout the balance of this chapter that your organization has vision, a mission, and value statements. Having these three directions will significantly aid regional brand strategies. I will focus on the following terms and areas of concentration to help bring the process of developing regional brand strategies to life.*

Principles (Step 4)

Principles are fundamental truths or assumptions, which serve as the framework for the way you conduct business. Every business plan, whether it be relevant to regional marketing or not, should be true to operating principles.

Objectives (Step 5)

Objectives are a strategic position to be obtained or a purpose to be achieved. As much as the vision and values collectively determine why the organization does something, objectives are the organization's "whats." The objective is the direction the organization chooses to go.

Goals (Step 6)

Goals are the end towards which effort is directed. Goals dimensionalize the objective and are recognized by the characteristics of specific, measurable, achievable, and compatible (SMAC). While it is very important for goals to be specific, measurable, and achievable, it is critical that they are also compatible. In fact, the one necessity of this regional planning model is that it be faithful to itself and congruent, where practical, with the overall national brand strategy. The national brand strategy should also be the harmonious collection of the various functional strategies that affect the brand.

Strategy (Step 7)

Strategies and tactics are the "hows" of the plan. A strategy is a careful plan or method. Strategies are sets of choices in key business areas, which, like most elements, are allowed and expected to change over time. They must be allowed to have a level of flexible integrity. A brand often has a series of strategies. It is also very appropriate for different corporate functions to develop their own specific strategies that must align and contribute to the overall organizational or regional strategic plan. The strategy is the backbone of the planning model that we will review shortly. It is also important to capture all assumptions in this step. The understanding of assumptions is so vital that it could be called Step 7A.

Tactics (Step 8)

Tactics are specific plans and action steps to help accomplish the strategy, which, if achieved, attains the end result, or goal. Without guidance, most people go right to the tactics phase of the model.

Measures (Step 9)

Measures are quantitative benchmarks against which to routinely check your overall progress.

Critique and Review (Step 10)

Periodic and *final* program reviews are essential to recognize assumption, and condition changes, as well as results.

PRINCIPLES FOR REGIONAL BRAND STRATEGIES

Principle 1: Do Not Have a Lot of Regional Brand Strategies

My region had approximately 20 different submarkets. I had approximately 20 different products that I represented. If you multiply these, the upside potential existed for approximately 400 slightly different regional brand strategies. Obviously, the development and deployment of this many strategies would have, in effect, crippled the organization. This is the classic example, mentioned previously, of "to do everything is to do nothing." Instead, I looked at the markets and respective brands and used an opportunities grid shown in Figure 11–1.

When filling out the Regional Opportunities Prioritizer, I first selected the top five priorities within each district. I had five districts in my division/region. I went through the process with each of the district management teams. Since they, of course, had done homework before the priority setting session, the process generally went very smoothly. After we developed the five top opportunities (the five were generally prioritized based upon annual incremental case gains), we then reviewed these opportunities more deeply. The headings are fairly self-explanatory, and I've already mentioned that annual incremental case gains were the initial driving consideration. We then reviewed the areas of success, cost in time, cost in dollars, and overall strategic timing. These four areas used a numerical rating scale. Importantly, number five, which is in the middle of the scale and represents neutral, was a rating that was not allowed to be assigned. I wanted people to come down on either side of the fence, yes or no, and not squarely on the fence.

FIGURE 11–1
Regional Opportunities Prioritizer

Opportunity	Annual Incremental Sales	Probability of Success 1 = High 10 = None	Cost: Sales and Marketing Time 1 = High 10 = Low	Cost: Actual Dollars 1 = High 10 = Low	Timing 1 = Great 10 = Terrible	C.D.I. B.D.I.	Other Factors
1.							
2.							
3.							
4.							
5.							

Category Development Index (C.D.I.)

The next area of consideration was the Category Development Index (C.D.I.) and the Business Development Index (B.D.I.)! These variables are extremely important. The Category Development Index is determined by first combining annual category sales of all the individual markets. In this case, the market is the whole United States. The overall category is then divided by the number of measured markets to get an average. In the United States, there are about 30 key markets for most consumer goods. Each individual market, then, is rated against the average U.S. category market. You can do this analysis if you have data in almost any category such as automobiles, fast-food sales, paint, hula hoops, or ketchup. Let's stay with the ketchup example for a moment. If you know the average market size for ketchup nationally, you then, as mentioned, can rank all of your individual markets against the average category size.

Business Development Index (B.D.I.)

Now, take your own company's business in the ketchup category and divide that total business by the number of markets. Then, as you did with category development, you measure each market against the average market size. Then, you easily index the various markets against the average to understand how your business is doing within each market.

Application

Once you have both the category development and the business development numbers, look for situations that have a high category development index and a low (your own) business development index. When you find this relationship, you can quickly tell that you are underdeveloped in a strongly developed market. This generally signals a significant business opportunity for you to pursue. You should not do this blindly, however, because it is also very important for you to attempt to maintain your presence in markets that are high category development and high (your own) Business Development Index.

The last column should be reserved for what I would call other factors. Other factors might be a new product introduction or business aberration such as Evian faced when Perrier had their product quality problem. I am in no way suggesting that Evian went through this analysis, but if I were Evian, I probably would have considered this other factor (significant Perrier product problem) and adjusted my business plans to capture sales and share.

After I went through this process for five opportunities, I fine-tuned the focus to the two best opportunities in each market. It happened that the two best opportunities were the same for all five of my districts. This is not always the case, though, because two of the five districts had a third opportunity that was a virtual tie with their second most appropriate choice. In this case, I simply asked the districts if they wanted to add a third opportunity to their menu.

Principle 2: Reviewing the Marketing Assessment Process (MAP)

You need to really gain an understanding of the competition, consumer, customer, your turf, and yourself. By going through the Marketing Assessment Process, you critically assess all the areas on the Regional Opportunities Prioritizer.

Principle 3: Align with National Strategies (if Possible)

Before you make your regional strategic choices, make sure you have a full understanding of the national brand strategies and plans. It is important for you to search and then reapply. This is in contrast to continually reinventing the wheel. Likely, there's a chance that a good central brand organization has taken into consideration various regional opportunities. In fact, it is not uncommon for good marketers to choose a region as a focus and key element of an overall national brand strategy. Once you have developed your opportunities grid, try to align wherever possible with a national plan. Reasonable congruence between plans is important. However, sometimes this is not possible because one district's primary regional brand opportunity may be a minimal consideration to the central brand organization's national plan. When this happens, it is important for the regional marketing organization to negotiate with the central brand organization. If the regional organization believes strongly enough in the particular opportunity, then as long as they are empowered, blessed, and financed, they should have a reasonable chance to have their point of view accepted and thus integrated into the national marketing program. It is important to remember that both organizations are on the same team, and this is not a battle. This should be, as much as possible, participatory democracy kept on a mature level. If there is disharmony, then it is incumbent for general management to arbitrate and make the final decision. This general management "safety net" should hardly ever be used but is important so that you protect the long-term integrity of the brand. It is also important for general management not to make a vague decision. Either you have a regional brand strategy or you don't. There should be no such thing as a "wink and blink" type plan.

TEN-STEP REGIONAL BRAND STRATEGY MODEL

Figure 11–2 is my best effort to define all the steps of the process that I have used over these past years to develop regional brand strategies. Additionally, this model works *very* well for plan development in almost all areas of business.

The first four steps—vision, mission, values, and principles—are preconditions. Ideally, it is very important to spend time in these four areas. They add meaning, integrity, and attitude to your business plan. Steps five through eight are the business plan itself: the objectives, goals, strategies, and tactics. Importantly, you *can* develop successful business plans without

FIGURE 11–2
Ten-Step
Regional Brand Strategy Model

Preconditions		Beliefs & Truths		Business Plan				Conscience	
Abstract Future State	Purpose			What		How		Check-points	Post Strategy Analysis
						Method	Sub-Method		
V I S I O N	M I S S I O N	V A L U E S	P R I N C I P L E S	O B J E C T I V E S	G O A L S	S T R A T E G I E S	T A C T I C S	M E A S U R E S	C R I T I Q U E A N D R E V I E W
Step 1	Step 2	Step 3	Step 4	Step 5	Step 6	Step 7	Step 8	Step 9	Step 10
Imagine! How would you like it to be?	Specific statement of purpose.	What you stand for. Your corporate integrity or lack thereof.		General direction.	Specific direction.	*Method* General plan. Capture assumptions.	*Sub-Method* Detailed plan.	Are we winning or losing?	What worked? What didn't?

formalizing your point of view on the preconditions. Person-ally, I would not recommend it, but I have done this with indi-vidual brands in individual markets where we didn't have the time and resources to develop quality preconditions. We just had a general sense of the type of business people we were, dis-cussed our personal and professional attitudes, and then enacted the business plan.

Steps 9 and 10 are what I call the model's conscience. Specifically, they are a periodic ongoing review of how the business plan is progressing compared to its previously agreed-upon measures. Once the review period is done (say, a fiscal year) a post-strategy analysis is conducted. If you choose, you can analyze your progress via these checkpoint measurements quarterly so that, in effect, you have a rolling analysis process. The rolling process allows you to continually replenish your strategic model and doesn't cause you to abruptly end in a stop-start fashion. To add understanding to this model, I will review two examples.

The first is a very shallow, nonbusiness example. It is important to look at examples analogously so that we have a general understanding of the model before we get into the details.

Head West

The first example is what could have been developed if one of our early American pioneers had the rare opportunity to buy *The Complete Guide to Regional Marketing*.

Step 1: Vision—We join our Philadelphia blacksmith Ken Maddox in the mid-1800s. Ken has a vision. That vision is a little abstract and vague, but he believes there is a better life out west.

Step 2: Mission—Ken's mission is to work hard at his job so that he can save enough money to provide a better life for him-self and his family.

Step 3: Values—Ken's values consist of hard work, honesty, and fairness.

Step 4: Principles—He believes in traveling only during daylight and will travel five days straight without rest.

Step 5: Objective—Ken decides to head west!

Step 6: Goals—Ken estimates that he and his family will arrive on the shores of the Pacific Ocean in the California territory one year from the time he leaves.

Step 7: Strategies—Ken believes that since he will be bringing his family along, he must travel west via wagon.

Step 8: Tactics—For safety reasons, Ken decides to approach other people and form a wagon train. He also elects to take a generally southern route to avoid harsh weather wherever possible. Ken decides to rig a sail for his wagon to take advantage of any favorable breezes on the Plains.

Step 9: Measures—Ken has developed a specific plan so that he knows where he should be every 50 days to achieve his ultimate goal of arriving on the Pacific Coast in one year.

Step 10: Critique/Assessment—Every time Ken approaches one of his measurement checkpoints, he evaluates how he is doing compared with his overall objective. Once Ken arrives, he will have time to reflect on his long journey. After reflection, he could head back east to lead other wagon trains (for profit) or stay and prosper on his land.

A BUSINESS EXAMPLE

Background

This business example will focus on steps five through eight of the Regional Brand Strategy Model. As mentioned previously, steps 1 through 4 are preconditions that should be addressed by the overall organization. If, for whatever reasons, the organization has not attended to these business conditions, then regional brand strategies can still be developed and executed. Focusing on steps 5 through 8 is the short-form approach to this model. Steps 9 and 10 will be mentioned but not focused on.

The business example I will use is found in the consumer packaged goods business. This model, though, is universal to all business categories. The model should be customized in steps seven and eight to the type of business that you are involved with. The way you do this is by focusing on what are called core tasks. Core tasks are the primary focus areas specific to your business category. For example, the primary core task areas are called sales and marketing controllables. The controllables are:

1. Distribution.
2. Price.
3. Merchandising.
4. Shelf.
5. Advertising.

If you are engaged in the sales and marketing of financial service products, airline travel, fast-food service, or leasing office space, you will probably have different core task areas. For example, these businesses just mentioned will not be concerned with shelf space as a core task focus area.

Situation

XYZ brand competes with two other primary national competitors and one strong regional competitor in the chocolate syrup category. Our particular XYZ brand is currently the second largest in both sales and share in a very high category development market. Our business development on XYZ brand is below average national levels; therefore, a significant opportunity exists. Nationally, XYZ chocolate syrup is the largest in both share and sales. Both the regional marketing and sales organizations, as well as the central sales and marketing organizations, agree that progress needs to be made in this particular region.

> *Author's Note: It would take several pages to identify all the business variables and conditions. It is my intent here to simply express the format of the business plan.*

As mentioned before, it is critical for the regional organization to conduct the regional priorities review as well as the marketing assessment process. Once these two processes have been conducted, there should be sufficient information available to construct the plan. A possible plan for the previously mentioned XYZ chocolate syrup business is as follows:

Objective: To have XYZ chocolate syrup become the number one total sales dollar volume chocolate syrup brand in the region.

Goal: To double XYZ's shipments within three years.

Author's note: You could choose to integrate share and profit criteria into this goal statement to provide further direction.

General Strategies:

1. Incremental effort will be focused against the 64-ounce large size.
2. Tolerate no more than a 10 percent slippage in sales on the existing smaller 16- and 32-ounce sizes.

Tactics (Aligned within core task areas):

1. *Distribution*—(A) Fill all existing 64-oz. distribution opportunities. (B) Fill all practical (other size) distribution opportunities.

2. *Price*

a. Parity cost and retail pricing compared to the number one brand on both the 16- and 32-ounce size.

b. Cost to a five percent pricing advantage every day on the shelf and cost at least to a 10 percent advantage during sale periods on the 64 ounce size compared to the number one brand.

3. *Merchandising*

a. Maintain previous-year merchandising levels on both the 16- and 32-ounce sizes.

b. Increase merchandising frequency on the 64-ounce size to a level of two incremental events per account in the region.

4. *Shelf*—Move from current 15 percent of category shelf space to 25 percent using a technology-driven shelf presentation model.
5. *Advertising*
   a. Increase the gross rating point weight by 50 percent on national copy within this region.
   b. Develop and deploy a regional radio program during the first half of the fiscal year targeted towards the 64-ounce size. Target and deploy a billboard program during the second half of the fiscal year, also targeted towards the 64-ounce size. (Special note: Both of these regional advertising executions could possibly be customer-ized to accounts to help achieve the merchandising tactical plan to secure two larger size [64-ounce] merchandising opportunities.)

Assumptions/Issues

Every business plan should be framed within various business assumptions and issues. In the XYZ chocolate syrup scenario, various assumptions should be established. If these assumptions change, they would lead toward an adjustment in the plan. A classic example is in the area of competitive pricing and merchandising. If you understand that the competition in the previous year has had five merchandising events and has costed their products to certain levels, this is a starting point. However, should competition choose to alter this pattern, whether on their own or in reaction to XYZ's initiatives, then the playing field will have been either subtly or substantially changed compared with the time when you developed the plan. Therefore, it is important to "model in" a few contingency plans based upon the way you believe competition will react. Additionally, your target competitor, in this case the number one leading chocolate syrup brand, may perform predictably during your initiative. However, one of the other brands, whether it be the other national or the regional brand, may react so extremely that you need either to react to the (hopefully) aberration or adjust your volume or spending commitments due to this unforeseen business condition.

Measures/Critique/Review

Since this is a three-year plan, you need to plot a three-year measurement and critique process. Measurements should be developed to monitor your success against the overall goals, strategies, and particular core-task tactics. The post-strategy analysis is really an ongoing (monthly, quarterly—you decide) review.

If you do not revisit your plan faithfully and frequently, then you will either ultimately fail or not understand why you have succeeded. Faithfulness to this plan is critical so that the clash-of-cultures issue does not arise. Regional sales organizations have frequently embarked upon glorious (theoretically blessed) plans that were supposed to be long-term. However, for a variety of reasons three-year plans often become one-year plans, and the regional sales organization develops an acute case of cynicism. The same thing also happens to brand organizations wherein regional sales departments, for a variety of reasons (overall volume problems or new item initiatives), abandon or lose their interest in the plan. A way to help manage this is by a contract.

CONTRACTING

The absence of contracts (internal) is a fundamental weakness in traditional business organizations. We often use contracts to bind agreements and commitments with external customers, yet rarely do we use them in-house. Personally, I do not favor creating mountains of paper and contracts that are 25-pages long. However, a one-page contract or even signature blocks on the regional business plan can bind managers to a certain starting point, a plan, and a desired end-result. Therefore, I recommend that each regional business plan that is developed, since it is usually an agreement between centralized and decentralized sales and marketing organizations, be signed in triplicate. One signatory should be the regional owner; the next signatory should be the central office owner; and the third signatory should be the general manager of the department. You may want to put financial cost parameters around this process, so that general managers aren't spending time signing-off on low-cost programs.

SUMMARY

It is important to manage the whole process of regional brand strategies with a level of sensibility. As mentioned previously, I am not suggesting that every region should have a strategy for every brand. However, I believe that national brand programs usually attend to the majority of business opportunities and needs that exist. However, to move your businesses ahead, a recognition and plan to deal with regional opportunities need to be put in place. The development and deployment of regional brand strategies is the most important leadership function that a regional marketing manager can perform. Regional marketers should also become involved in the management of the plan, but there are also central office and regional sales types that will share in the management.

When developing regional brand strategies, you need to intimately know the consumer from an advertising perspective and the customer from a sales perspective. As mentioned in Chapter nine, there is no singular more important business direction. The implementation of that belief takes place in the area of customer-ized marketing. Customer-ized marketing is the second leg of what I consider to be ultimate regional marketing. When reviewing the next chapter, "Customer-ized Marketing," think particularly about how individual lead account strategies can be integrated back into the Regional Brand Strategy Model.

SUMMARY CHECKLIST

1. *Do you have two or three focused regional brand strategies? Do you have so many brand strategies that they resemble the flavor-of-the-month club?*

2. *Are you comfortable with your review of the Marketing Assessment Process (MAP)?*

3. *Are your primary regional brand strategies compatible with the national brand strategies?*

4. *Does your overall organization have a vision, a mission statement, and values? What about operating principles?*

5. *Have you developed objectives, goals, strategies, and tactics for your business plan?*

6. *Have you developed measurements/criteria for success? Do you have an ongoing critique and review process in place? Have you built in a post-program critique and review process?*

7. *Have you quantified the assumptions and issues that exist before you embark on your regional brand strategy plan? If the assumptions and issues change during the process of the strategy implementation, does your organization have flexibility to change your plan?*

8. *Do you use internal contracting?*

9. *Have you agreed upon a corporate language so that people (all disciplines) understand what's expected of each step of the plan?*

Chapter Twelve

Customer-ized Marketing

INTRODUCTION

Customer-ized marketing takes regional marketing to the next step. By that, I mean that the external customer is treated as the primary subset or focus of the region.

To develop a customer-ized marketing approach within a region, it is very important to understand the regional customers. I have discussed customers earlier in the book, and, for clarification's sake, I am addressing a company's external customers. In my universe, that means a direct manufacturer selling to a retail operation. The retail operation in turn sells to the ultimate consumer. Many businesses don't interact this way, but I still believe that the attitude is a healthy one whether you have a traditionally channeled relationship or not.

Customer-ized marketing takes both a macro and a micro approach.

MACRO APPROACH

This style recognizes who the primary business customers are within a region. It is not uncommon in the consumer packaged goods business to have as many as 15 key customers in a region with varying degrees of business control. It is very difficult (manufacturers have tried for years) to make all of these customers within a region happy with every marketing and sales program. In fact, it is difficult at any one point in time to totally satisfy even 50 percent of this customer panel. The macro approach that I suggest recognizes the two or three strongest business influencers in a particular region and tries to isolate the business variables and approaches that these two or three customers have in common. For example, when you introduce a new item, do the two or three largest customers demand high levels of television gross rating points? Do the two or three primary customers dislike it when coupons are used on a regular basis? It is important to seek an understanding of what works for the primary customers and then try to ethically develop a marketing program that will ensure success at these lead businesses, yet treat all customers fairly.

I can't overstate the issue of fairness. If sellers cannot develop programs that are equitable to *all* retailers, then they should not prostitute themselves to develop unfair programs.

Developing programs for the two or three lead customers in a market is not unfavorable to the balance of the customer panel as long as it is fair and equitable. In fact, it is initially startling to understand that the other customers in the region understand that business is business, and as long as they're being treated equitably on a fair-share basis, they will not expect nor ask for more.

Identifying the two or three lead accounts in a market should not be done *just* by share of business. In a market that I am familiar with, there were about five different customers that all represented about 10 percent of the actual region's business. Upon closer examination, though, one could clearly identify two or three that were actually the lead customers in the region based upon swiftness to market with the new items and regional pricing practices. Then, you can also figure out over time which customers play follow-the-leader and which customers are the true leaders. Once you identify these true leaders, you can quickly understand that a customer, representing only 10 percent of the overall business, can easily influence 40 to 50 percent of the overall business. My caution is to thoroughly review the intercustomer relationships and don't just make a decision on absolute business volume at the present.

A national organization would be well advised to have all markets conduct this process. Once you do this, you will wake up to the fact that there are probably 50 customers nationally that collectively represent, or influence, close to a majority of your business. It is really the old "20 percent of the effort gets you 80 percent of the result" rule. I know for a fact that this focus or formula relates to many more industries than the consumer packaged-goods categories. In fact, if you talk with airlines and hotels, you will find that the majority of the best operators in those industries clearly understand which corporate clients provide them regionally with the most business.

This macro approach does not provide for a perfect business order. However, it does significantly enhance the organization's ability to focus on the big opportunities.

MICRO APPROACH

Envision, if you will, going to the eye doctor's office and having a routine eye exam. The ophthalmologist hooks you up to the same machine that we've all been hooked up to, where you put your chin in a rest and eerie goggles take their position in front of your eyes. The ophthalmologist starts with a blurry lens and continually changes the lens choice. As this happens, your vision sequentially becomes clearer. Analogously, what we've done here is recognize that national mass marketing has worked for quite some time, but it is the blurry lens. We have shifted to several types of smaller focused marketing styles (special events, ethnic, micro, and others). Our vision has finally started to gain clarity when we view the world through the regional lens. We are now trying to focus more from that regional lens and are zeroing in on the top two or three accounts in a region. From that lens, we now progress to an ultimately finer magnification called the individual account. Critics would argue that the ultimate view should be to own a thorough understanding of the end user or the consumer. I agree with that and believe that both the sales and marketing organizations should approach the business on parallel paths. As stated earlier in this book, the advertiser should own an understanding of the consumer, and the sales function should own an understanding of the customer. Since both sales and marketing have over the years tried to "polish" the consumer focus with varying degrees of success, it is now time to try to polish the approach toward the customer.

If you remember the Ten-Step Regional Brand Strategy Model, we are now focusing on what I call method marketing. In a broad sense, we are evolving from an overall strategy of primary customer focus within a region to a micro approach that zeros in on independent relationships with the two or three lead regional accounts. In essence, we are moving to a state of customer teaming or partnering.

When I became involved with the customer team approach, I treated the word *team* as a nasty four-letter word. This is not uncommon, because most sales and marketing organizations have attracted some well-intentioned individualists. It was always considered noble and value-added in recruiting when we found people who were involved in teams, but we were really trying to recruit the team captains and/or leaders. When you collectively assemble a group of chiefs, it takes special training and time to develop a good team. When you ask these people to partner with customers in formal or informal team settings, that demands paradigm shifts. Most organizations on the front end are not used to teaming with customers, especially if you are from a background of having a win-lose relationship with customers. Of course, the first thing that has to take place is a general shift in belief that we should only be involved with win-win programs. Once this major hurdle is overcome, then the playing field is level enough for a potentially productive customer-team relationship.

CUSTOMER TEAMS

I want to spend significant time here to enhance the overall micro focus on customer-ized marketing. The product of a micro customer-ized approach is the development and establishment of formal and informal customer business teams.

It is important to note that I have mentioned formal and informal teaming. Teaming is an attitude as much as it is a legitimate formal relationship. Teaming generally takes place more frequently on an informal basis with a general structure but no long-term charter. In fact, informal teams exist on an ad hoc basis. An example of teaming or partnership marketing on an informal basis is the buyers and sellers of a manufacturer and retailer getting together once per quarter to review the business and talk about future plans. Another example of an informal team attitude is for manufacturers to periodically discuss with retailers new item introductions before they happen. It is a sincere and valid attempt of the seller to extend to the buyer the courtesy of a preview of what is going to happen in the future. The seller then gets specific input as to how the new introduction effort would be received by the particular account. I have been involved in several of these sessions, and they are incredibly valuable. Interestingly, my involvement with customers on new items has happened only in the last couple of years. Some companies, however, have been engaged in this teaming approach for several years with significant business improvement because of it.

Teaming *as a concept* should be universally offered to all customers. All customers will not be receptive to the opportunity, and that is their choice. When you have several customers who are interested in teaming, it is important to have the trained resources available to allow for engagement if it is desired on both sides. The concept of teaming is fair and equitable if a region has a shared resource pool in the areas of technology and distribution as well as sales and marketing. Clearly, some teams should take priority over others for resource access. Again, this should be determined by who are the primary business customers in the region. However, it is important that if any customer wants to team, whether it be formal or informal, they be provided this opportunity based upon available resources.

If teams are to become part of the future customer relationship, then a few guidelines should be followed:

1. Don't establish teams because they are currently corporately sexy. Establish them where there is a significant business opportunity. The last time I checked, we are all employed to move our businesses ahead. Team when and if it makes sense for *all* involved.

2. As with any organization, this combined group should have both organizations' top-to-top- management consensus and blessing.

3. Each team should have two leaders, one from the customer and one from the supplier, who together will provide the direction and logistical support.

4. The team members should have a steering committee that helps establish the design process for building the team.

5. The team should meet frequently on the front end of process development and then meet when it is appropriate. Beware of unnecessary and pro forma meetings, because they serve to sour the overall process.

6. The teams should try to functionally line up. By that, I mean if the team in its design believes that product supply is critically important, then there should be a product supply person from both organizations. If a person cannot be provided, then at least the necessity for information on the function of product supply should be managed. Without individual members committed, there is the possibility that instant gratification will not be forthcoming. But if the teams' people can get back to the appropriate resources within their organizations, then the product-supply function can be serviced on a different level. Perhaps once every three months a product-supply person could visit the group and, on a less frequent basis, manage the functional needs. Of course, this is not a perfect plan, but at least it recognizes that there are functions beyond buying and selling that can benefit from an overall team relationship. Importantly, I don't generally agree with part-time team members. However, if the product-supply function is not an ongoing need, then this visiting relationship is acceptable.

7. Beyond the design process, it is important for functional strategies to be developed that should blossom into overall team strategies. It is clearly up to the comfort zone of the team members about how deeply they want to get into the process, but they could, in a mature sense, follow the Ten-Step Regional Brand Strategy Model. This model, as mentioned before, has universal application and can be used to guide and manage the overall business relationship of the team.

8. Make sure that the teaming process and ongoing relationship is not just business-directed. Try to inject some fun in the process so that the team can merge personally. Ultimately, most organizations in the long term survive on the integrity of the systems that exist. However, in the short term, as these systems and relationships are developing, it is important for people to understand one another and to try to enjoy the relationship that they are involved with. Fun, a sense of humor, and enjoyment will go a long way during the initial phases of this relationship and could set the stage for a very comfortable relationship for years to come.

9. Beware of the hostage syndrome. Early in a teaming relationship that I was involved with, my customer counterpart warned me one day to remember that we were friends but not married. This caught me by surprise, and I was initially tempted to take this personally. However, upon further examination, what this person was saying was fundamentally correct. He suggested that while we were getting very cozy personally and professionally and everything was working smoothly, we still had to remember that we worked for different companies. This comment served to be very prophetic to me, when I worked in a position with Procter & Gamble's sales merchandising division at the headquarters location. I frequently interacted with the brand and sales. I also interacted

with traditional sales and sales that were involved with customer teams. On more than one occasion, my initial reaction based upon the customer-team sales request was, "Whose side are you on?" I believed that the seller had become the hostage of the team. Our system was being stretched to accommodate the wishes of the teams to a level that was approaching fantasy. This friction was not even a cultural one. Instead, we were both salespeople trying to pursue our mutually exclusive points of view. Confusion will exist on the front end of most relationships, but I believe there is a way to generally manage towards reality and reasonableness.

A TEAMING WATCHOUT

I am an advocate of a practical team approach to most business situations and relationships. The key word is *practical*. Frequently well-intentioned people who favor the team approach export that experience to every facet of their operation. This isn't necessary. Go slow on teaming. If a group of people are an ad hoc committee or a governing board, don't call them a team. In fact, if I hear one more normal group of business people working on a project called a "leadership team," I'll probably scream.

Additionally, I strongly believe in up-front "on boarding" training whenever any new team is developed. But if the group is still receiving team-building training by about the tenth meeting, then they should disband because they have not learned their lessons well. "Overtraining" can hinder business results and give teams a bad name when they probably don't deserve it.

The team concept can work very well as long as we don't go overboard. One inherent watchout for teams (besides the out-of-control promulgation of them) is in the area of individual responsibility. By their very nature, teams share responsibility and reward. Teams, however, should not be so totally insulated that only the team leader feels responsible or, more importantly, is held responsible. The team's management and training is crucial. A lot of emphasis has been put on team bonding and cooperation, but individual responsibility and accountability should be equally emphasized.

Companies have been hiring high-powered individuals for quite some time. In essence, a lot of potential chiefs have been hired into management positions with very little attention paid to their conduct as team members. In the future, it would be wise to introduce some hiring criteria (if your organization believes in the team concept) to identify strong team players. These people are out there—we just need to ask the right questions to find them.

THREE LEVELS OF CUSTOMER RELATIONSHIPS

It is important to come to agreement that customer relationships can exist at three primary levels. It is important for strong relationships to be sequentially established at these levels instead of "end-running" them. The three levels of relationship are:

1. Dependable/trustworthy.
2. Accountable/reactive
3. Creative/proactive

- *Dependable/trustworthy*: We need to agree that in our customer relationships, it is first important to become dependable buyers and sellers. Until this basic level is achieved, we should tread carefully when dealing with being accountable and probably guard against jumping to being creative. Being a dependable partner is critical. My business experience started in the direct-store delivery business. No matter how much I attended to the profit and volume needs of my customers, I was always severely set back if I couldn't be dependable.

- *Accountable/reactive*: An accountable state can exist once we come to a mutual conclusion that we are doing very well via measurements as dependable partners.
- *Creative/proactive*: Once we agree that we are dependable and accountable, then and only then should we try to develop the relationship to the creative level.

What often happens in our mutually enthusiastic approach is that we recognize the charter to be dependable and accountable, but we find much more enjoyment in moving to the creative state. This should be guarded against.

It is because of this attempt to jump from level one to level three that the hostage syndromes start to set in. The hostage syndrome takes place when, over time, prisoners or hostages start to relate and pursue the points of the captors. On the front end of teaming relationships, it is very easy for sellers and suppliers to believe that they are the hostages and the buyers and customers are the captors. This relationship ultimately could and should not be further from the truth. Both operations have much to contribute, and they are both not so mutually dependent that they couldn't break off their relationship at any time.

TRUST IS IMPORTANT

One of the primary responsibilities of the teaming function is to quickly develop enduring trust among the participants. If trust exists, then the floodgates of improvement can be opened. The benefits of either formally or informally teaming with customers are overwhelming. You will recognize when this trust exists by your ability to let go and quit overmanaging. Letting go can pay big dividends, but is not without its risks and initial uneasiness. I finally let go when I came to the conclusion and agreement with a statement that was made by one of my customers. I was giving Fred Hartz, vice president of Shaw's Incorporated (a billion dollar food retailer) a quarterly business review. I was in the process of telling him how much money I had to invest behind my brands and his business for the next three months. Generally, I was telling him exactly what he had to do to earn the funds, which is very typical in the consumer packaged-goods business. He finally smiled at me and with no animosity said, "I wish you would trust us enough to let go and realize that we know how to sell your products through our stores better than you know how to sell your products through our stores." That one comment dramatically reshaped the way I interact with my customers. From that point forward, I generally let go of requirements. I trusted my customers to invest my resources to best advantage in our mutual businesses.

Of course, there's more to it than just letting go, since I have historically had many brands and therefore responsibility to many different masters. Since I don't want just one of my brands to totally outperform all the others at the expense of the remainder, clearly this approach does need some hand-holding and fine-tuning. However, the big decision for me was to let go and trust the customer. Regretfully, I have had a couple of negative and fairly predictable experiences with other customers. However, over the long haul, I can honestly say that letting go and having trust provides for a much more productive win-win relationship. Don't misunderstand this approach to be a total acquiescence on the seller's part. Sellers still must carefully craft good, solid, and balanced plans. The difference here is a mind-set that suggests that with good planning and coaching (versus requirements), a mutually beneficial arrangement can be developed.

The concept of teaming balanced with trust can help in most areas of business interaction. A primary area in which you should start to see early benefits to both partners is in the area of sales estimating and forecasting, which deals with out-of-stocks. Salespeople are usually notorious for being at *least* 10 percent, plus or minus, off their estimating process. Buyers, on the other hand, are usually within five percent regarding stock on hand that relates to their service level. In fact, if a buyer's service level slips, it is usually more a function of a manufacturer not being able to provide the product that was ordered. Just imagine the efficiencies that can be built back into the system that will help the buyer, the seller, and the consuming public by uniting the volume-forecasting process. If you move towards the teaming relationship, make service level one of your early focuses in the area of dependability.

SUMMARY

Whether you adopt a macro focus against two or three key customers (no teaming) or a micro focus wherein you team with target customers, both approaches make sense. In fact, merging both approaches (macro and micro) may be the best way to tackle a region. Customer-ized marketing or, as some will call it, trade marketing, is a formal recognition that the national mass marketing focus towards the customer and consumer does not always work. Consumer and customer-focused efforts should be compatible.

Sellers should keep in mind that they need to keep an ear open to their customers. If customers request certain programs that make sense in a win-win framework, then these programs should be pursued and the attempt to accommodate this relationship should not be misconstrued as giving in. On the reverse side, if a team comes forward with a specific request for merchandising dollars that will not be offered to all customers on a fair share basis, then this should be denied. The author of the plan should then be reviewed to see if that person is a hostage or just confused.

Customer-ized marketing recognizes the significant importance of the customer in the manufacturer-customer-consumer triad. It also recognizes that there are two ways to approach the consumer. The first is the traditional way of going directly to the consumer using general advertising methods. The second approach is to go through the customer to the consumer. While manufacturers have always gone through the customer to get to the consumer, it is the way that we have done it that needs to be addressed. Doing things that mutually benefit both relations is the way of the future and should lead to the development of strong alliances and partnerships—not legal partnerships, but operational relationships. The companies that understand this and pursue adding value to the seller-customer relationship will thrive in the years to come.

Lastly, partnerships and teaming should be grounded by market expectations and rewards. If the relationship gets too one-sided, try to resolve your differences. If this doesn't work, then get out of the relationship.

SUMMARY CHECKLIST

1. *Have you identified the two or three most instrumental accounts that are the real business influencers in a region?*

2. *Have you found the business common denominators among these accounts and built a plan for them and the rest of the region?*

3. *Does your company have enough conviction to abandon regional planning that is not equitable and fair to all accounts?*

4. *Do you want to move toward customer teams? If you do, are the resources available?*

5. *Are you capable of managing the risk of teams such as "hostage syndrome", team over proliferation, lack of individual responsibility, and overtraining?*

6. *Are you patient enough to allow for customer relations to evolve over time through the continuum of (1) dependable, (2) accountable, (3) creative?*

7. *Can you allow yourself to let go even a little bit to allow a spirit of trust and cooperation to settle in between your customer and you?*

Epilogue

As mentioned throughout the book, regional marketing is not a new style of marketing. However, companies do seem to be rapidly refinding this approach. As these companies progress with regional marketing, costly mistakes could be made. It is my hope that this book will aid companies, both domestically and internationally within all types of business categories, to manage regional marketing more productively.

In closing this book, I want to focus on eight key points:

1. Regional marketing, to be successful, must be embraced, blessed, and supported by company management. Regional marketers cannot be put in place and then orphaned.

2. Regional marketers should be carefully selected from both the sales and marketing disciplines. These people should be well trained, funded, and empowered. The position of regional marketing manager should be a desirable one and a "pass through" position towards upper sales and marketing management.

3. Companies should proactively recognize that the progression from totally centralized marketing to partially decentralized marketing does not come without its growing pains. Beyond that, if a company can comfortably integrate the sales and marketing cultures, then significant business growth should follow. Additionally, the managers that come from this interdisciplinary experience will be much better hybrid types and more well rounded to become future general managers.

4. Regional marketing to date has been a collection of experiences and tactics. Regional marketing of the future should be principle-centered.

5. The Marketing Assessment Process (MAP) should be taken seriously, not only in the area of regional marketing, but in business development in general.

6. Regional marketing always used to make the most sense to me when we worked hard to develop appropriate key regional brand strategies and then implemented these plans. The Ten-Step Regional Brand Strategy Model (similar to the Marketing Assessment Process) should supersede the discipline of regional marketing. This model has been around in bits and pieces for quite some time. I have spent time bringing the fragments together. This approach does produce good results when consciously and faithfully followed from step 1 through 10.

7. Customer-ized marketing and teaming (in moderation) really makes sense. My research indicates that several companies are engaging in this partnership marketing approach, and most report positive results.

8. Several companies have engaged in various levels of restructuring both their central and field organizations in recent years. As you move towards a regional marketing system, be aware that it may also be the right time to engage in a general sales and marketing restructure.

If your company moves towards regional marketing as an important business focus, take your time and behave conservatively. It is not one of the toughest business programs to deploy, but, on the other hand, you just can't have a series of meetings and then flip the switch and pretend you're doing regional marketing.

If you manage the development and deployment of regional marketing correctly, this marketing style has wonderful potential as either a primary style or an adjunct style for your company.

Regional marketing is catching on because customers and consumers like to be made to feel special. Regional marketing does that, because it is a sincere attempt to market to both of these audiences in their own backyards. Companies are integrating regional marketing into their business framework at a rapid velocity for one primary reason. That reason is regional marketing, if managed correctly, works!

Index

Other Business One Irwin Titles of Interest to You

MARKETING TO HOME-BASED BUSINESSES
Jeffrey P. Davidson

Over 34 million Americans are performing some or all of their work at home. Author Jeffrey P. Davidson shows marketers how to identify this often elusive segment of customers and gain their business. Davidson helps you acquire the knowledge, strategies, and techniques to effectively market to home-based businesses.

$39.95
ISBN: 1-55623-475-9

SAY IT WITH CHARTS
The Executive's Guide to Successful Presentations in the 1990s, Second Edition
Gene Zelazny

The Second Edition of *Say It With Charts* brings the task of choosing and using charts into the 1990s. Author Gene Zelazny expands his ideas on how to select the right chart for your presentation and shows you how to take advantage of new advances in computer graphics to create quality visuals for business presentations to small and large audiences.

$34.95
ISBN: 1-55623-447-3

THE NEW DIRECT MARKETING
How to Implement a Profit-Driven Database Marketing Strategy
David Shepard Associates

Construct, analyze, use, and evaluate the information in a marketing database to build sales and profits. The authors show you how to cost effectively acquire the primary and secondary data you need to identify and profile your best customers and prospects.

$52.50
ISBN: 1-55623-317-5

SELLING TO THE AFFLUENT
The Professional's Guide to Closing the Sales that Count

Dr. Thomas Stanley

Improve your closing percentage . . . and income. Dr. Stanley shows you how to approach wealthy prospects at the moment they are most likely to buy. In *Marketing to the Affluent* Stanley told you how to find them. Now he tells you how to sell to them.

$55.00
ISBN: 1-55623-418-X

MARKETING TO THE AFFLUENT

Dr. Thomas Stanley

A 1989 business book award finalist! Dr. Stanley shows you how to get the true demographics, psychographics, buying and patronage habits of the wealthy. Includes in-depth interviews with some of the nation's top sales and marketing professionals to help you pinpoint your best prospects.

$55.00
ISBN: 1-55623-105-9

Prices Subject to Change Without Notice.
Available in Fine Bookstores and Libraries Everywhere.